Thank you for choosing "The Book of Beautiful Birds" by Pretty Pine Press!

Would you like a **FREE e-BOOK?**

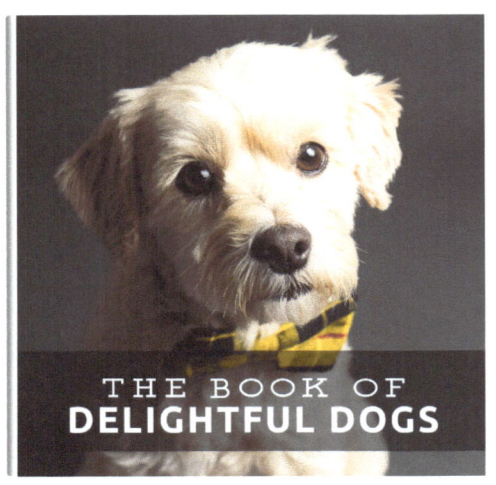

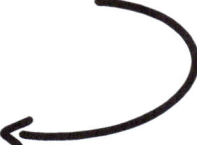

To claim your gift email us at prettypinepress@gmail.com

WE'D LOVE YOUR FEEDBACK!

Please let us know how we are doing by leaving us a review on Amazon.

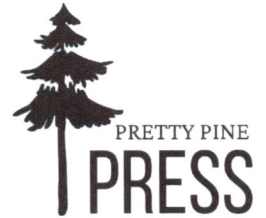

© 2020 Pretty Pine Press. All rights reserved.
No part of this publication may be reproduced, distributed, or transmitted in any form or by any means, including photocopying, recording, or other electronic or mechanical methods, without the prior written permission of the publisher, except in the case of brief quotations embodied in critical reviews and certain other noncommercial uses permitted by copyright law.

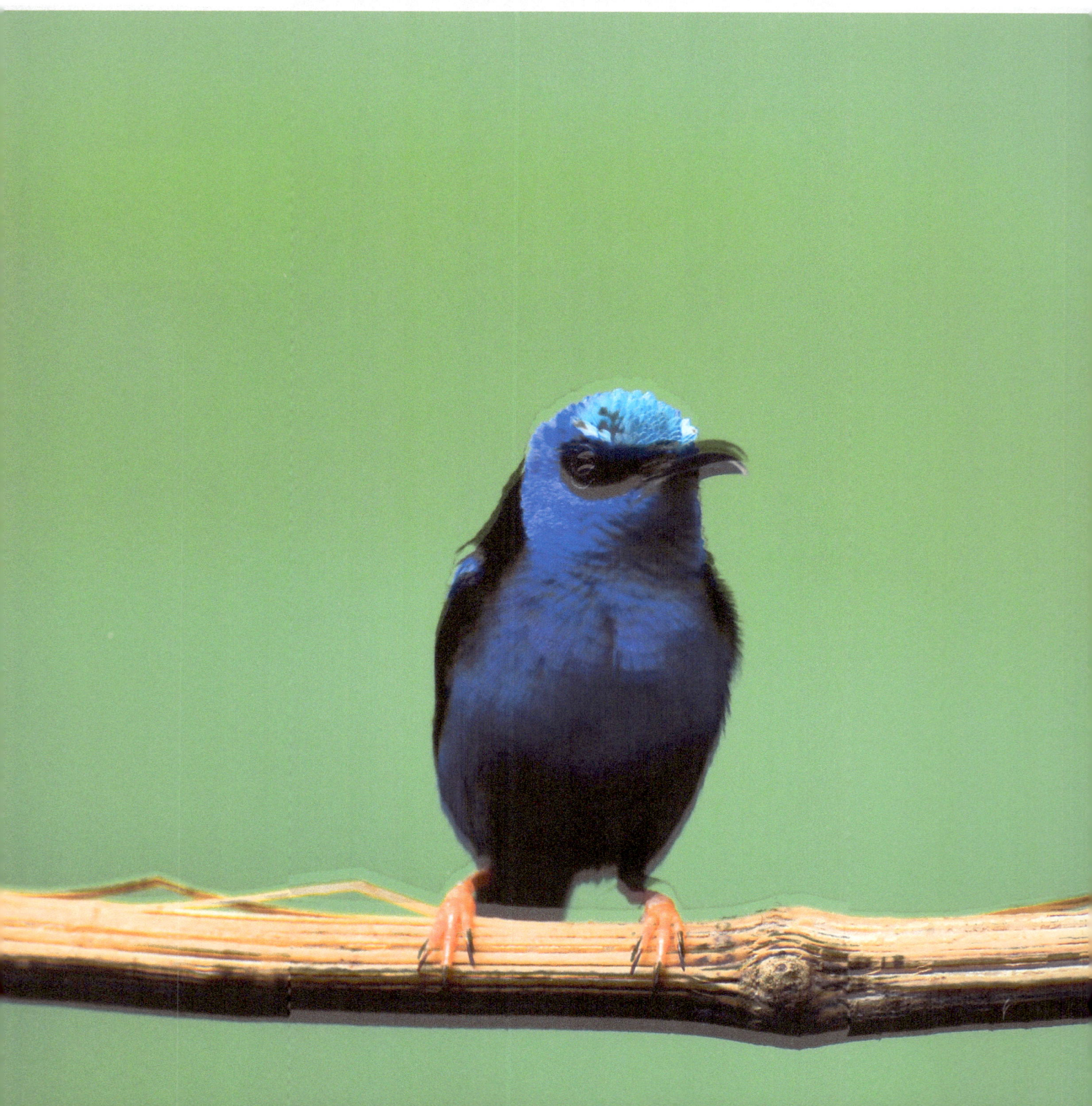

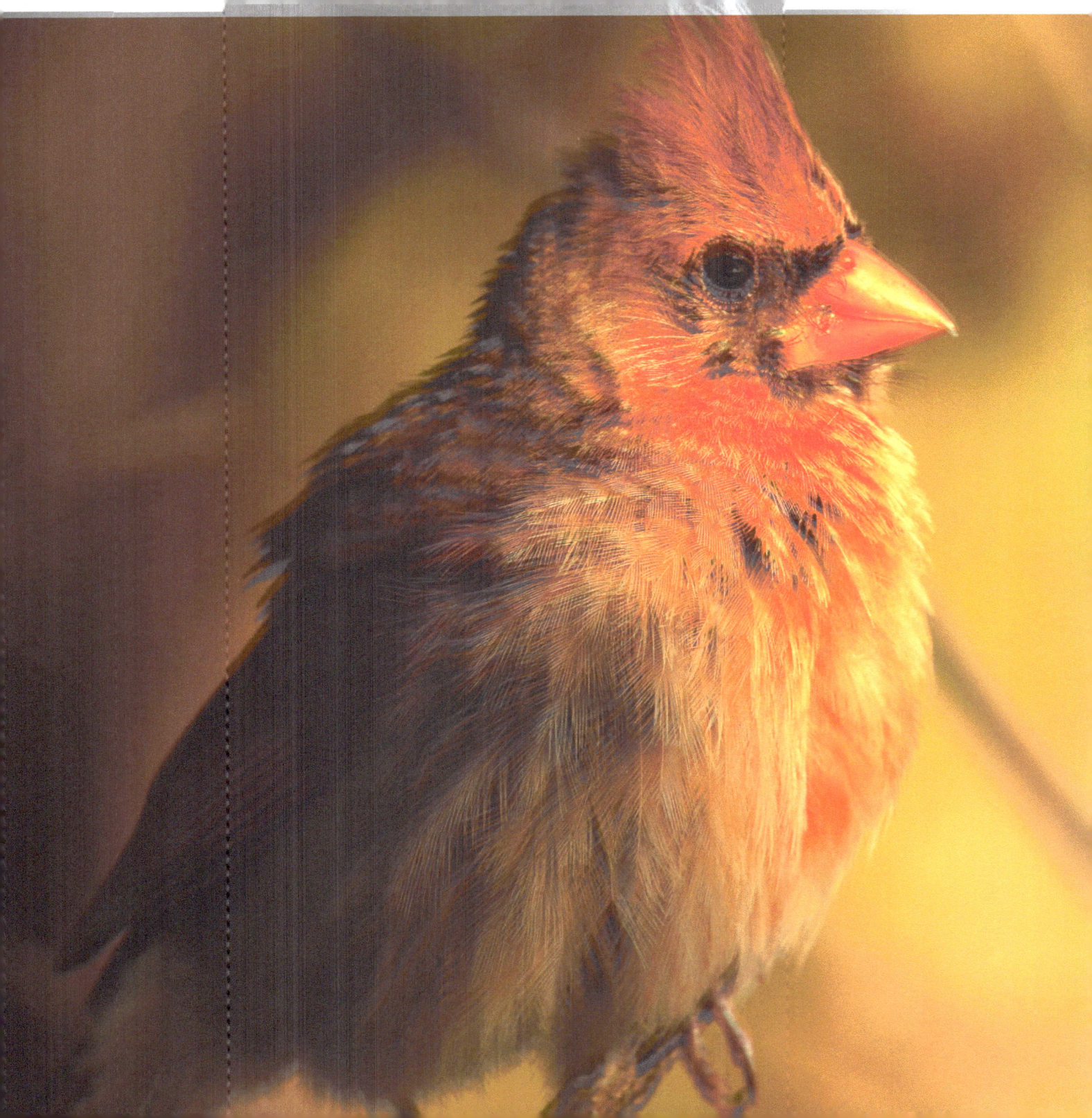

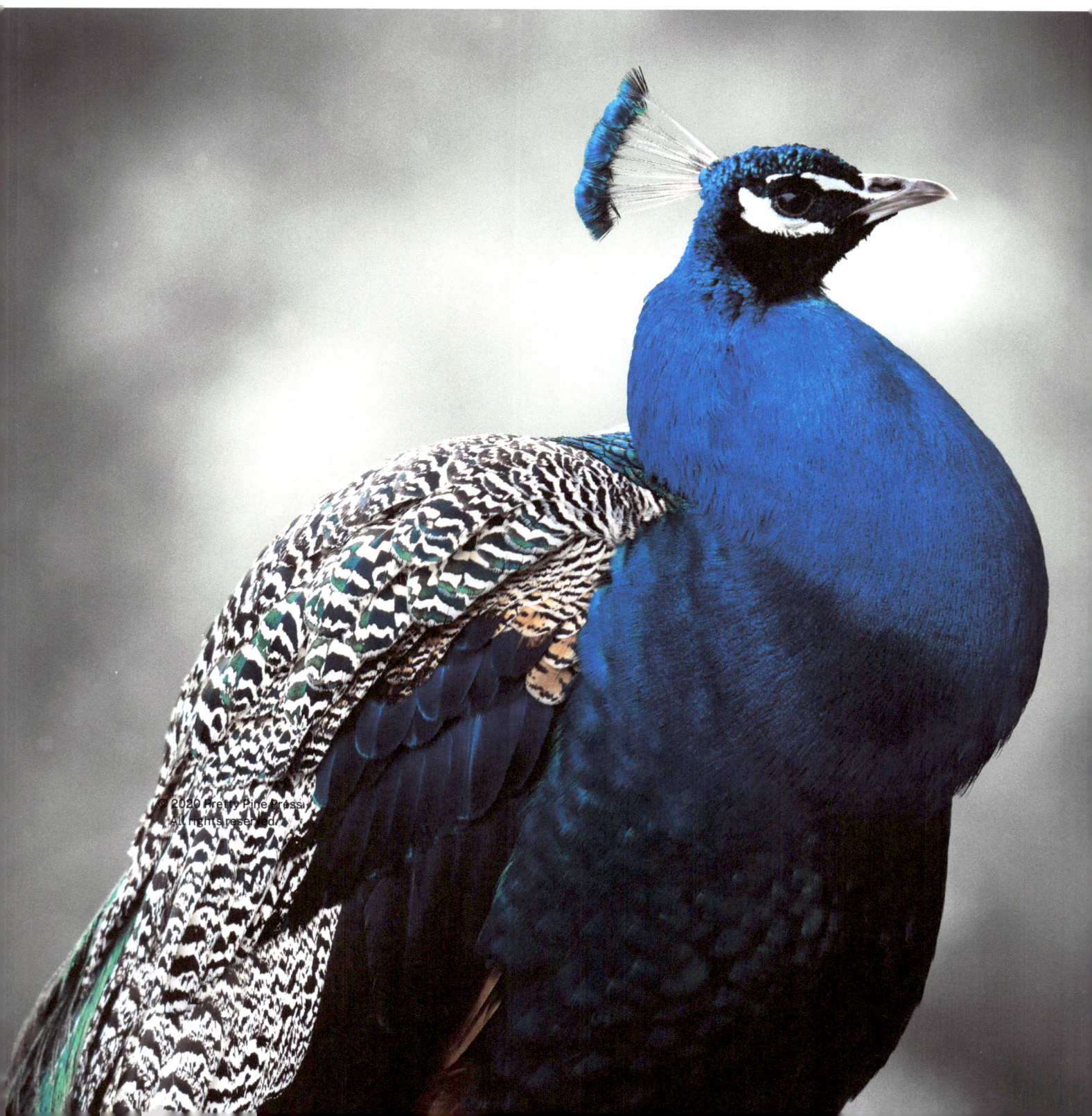

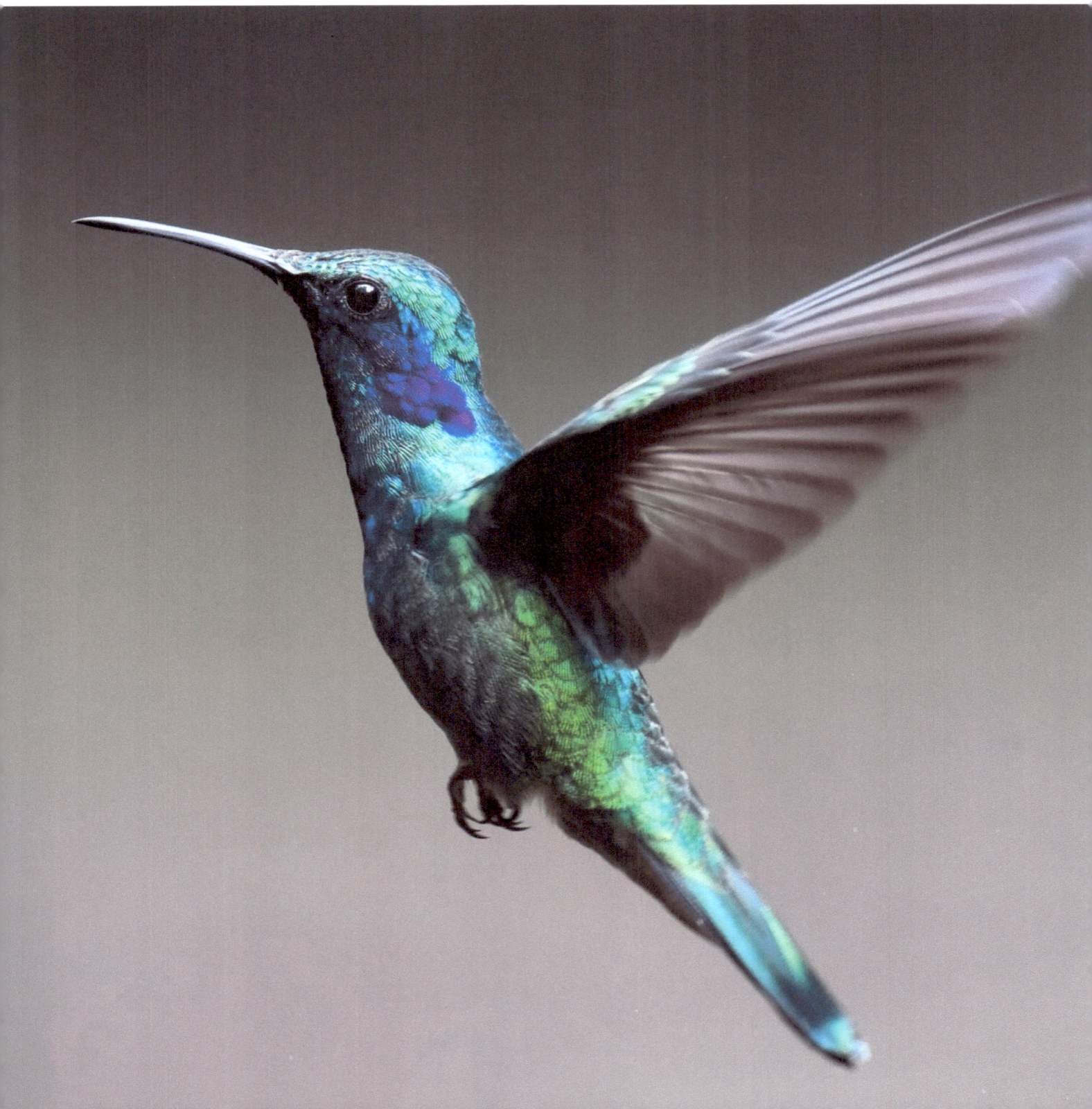

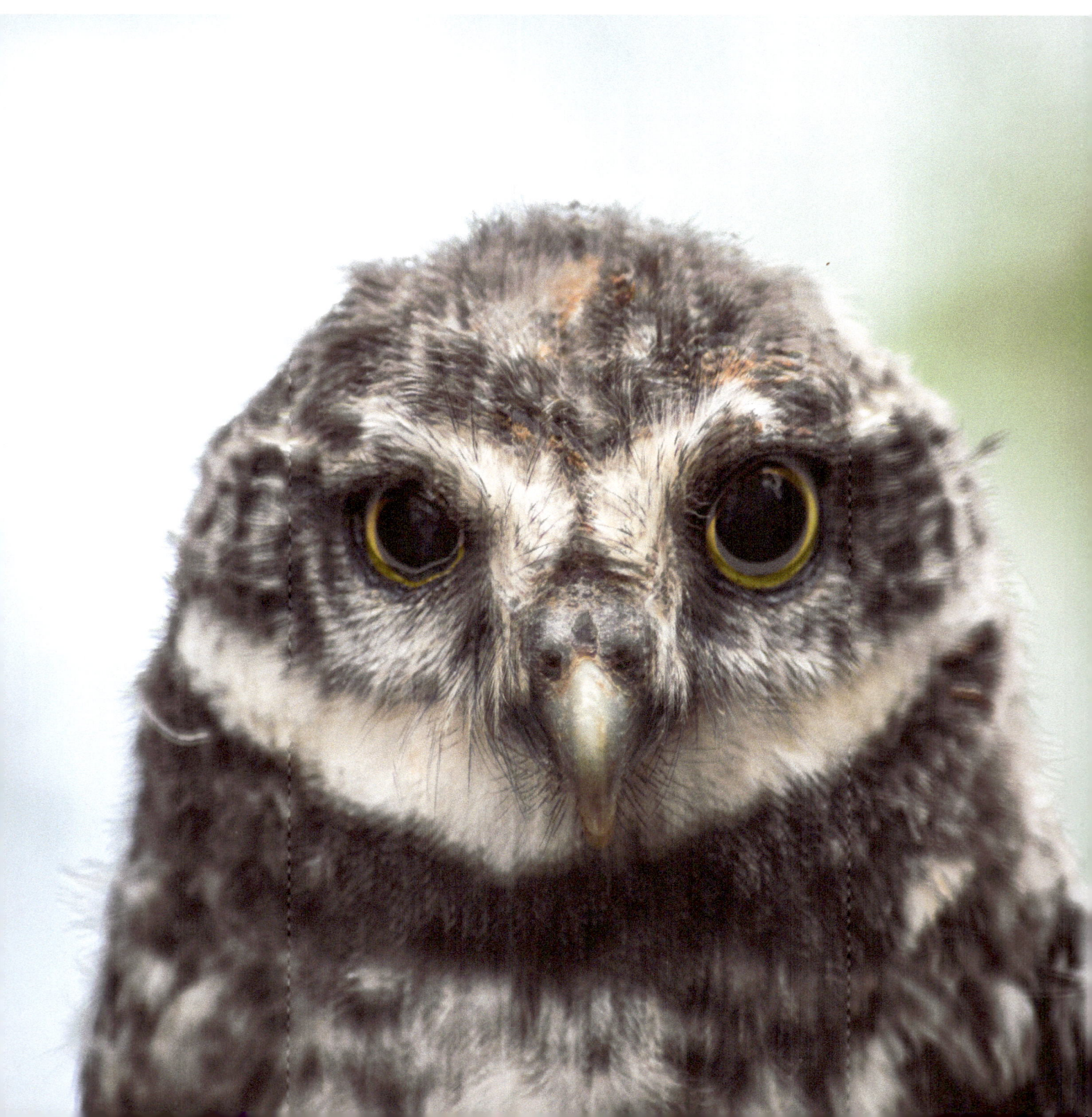

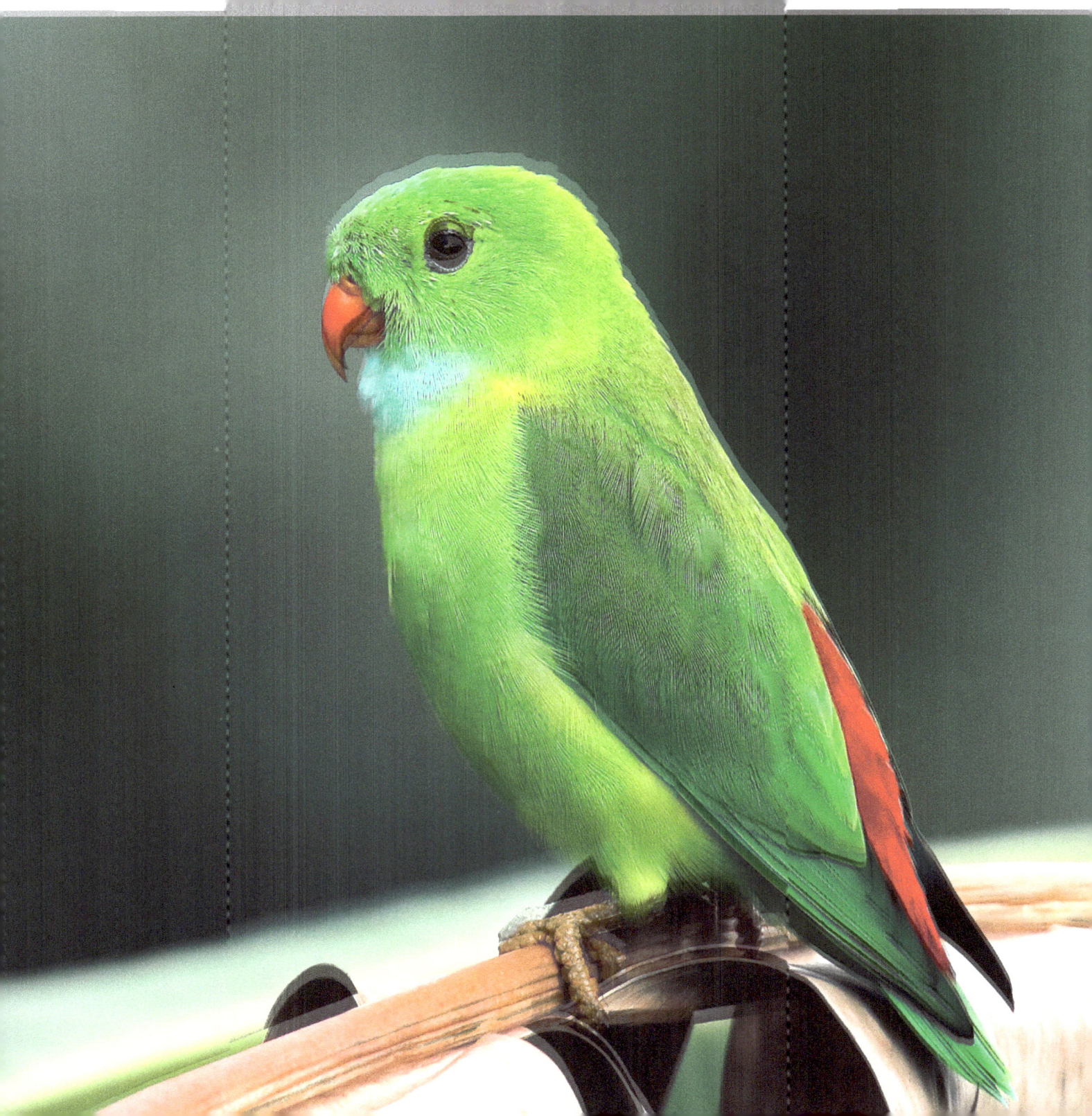

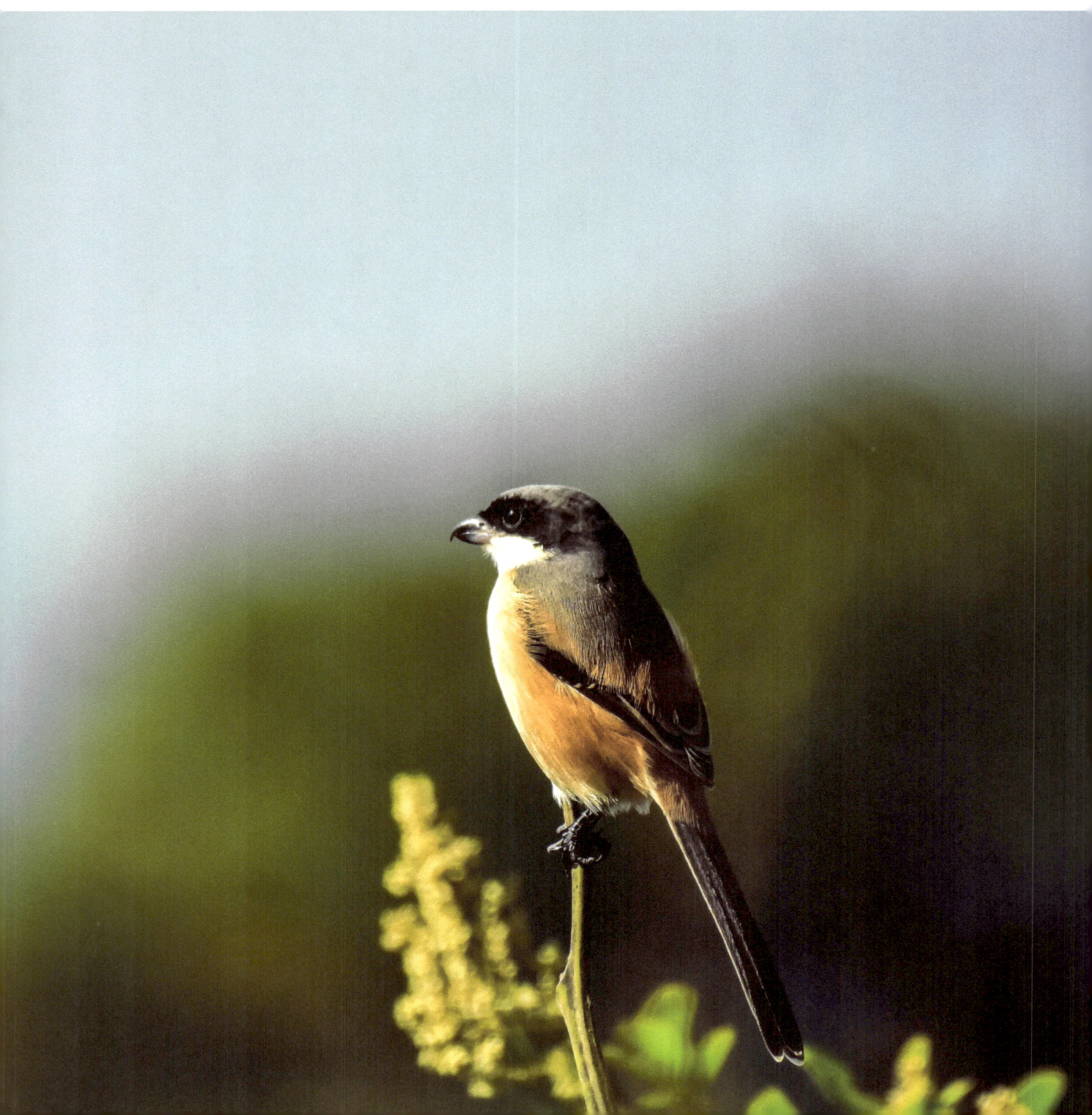

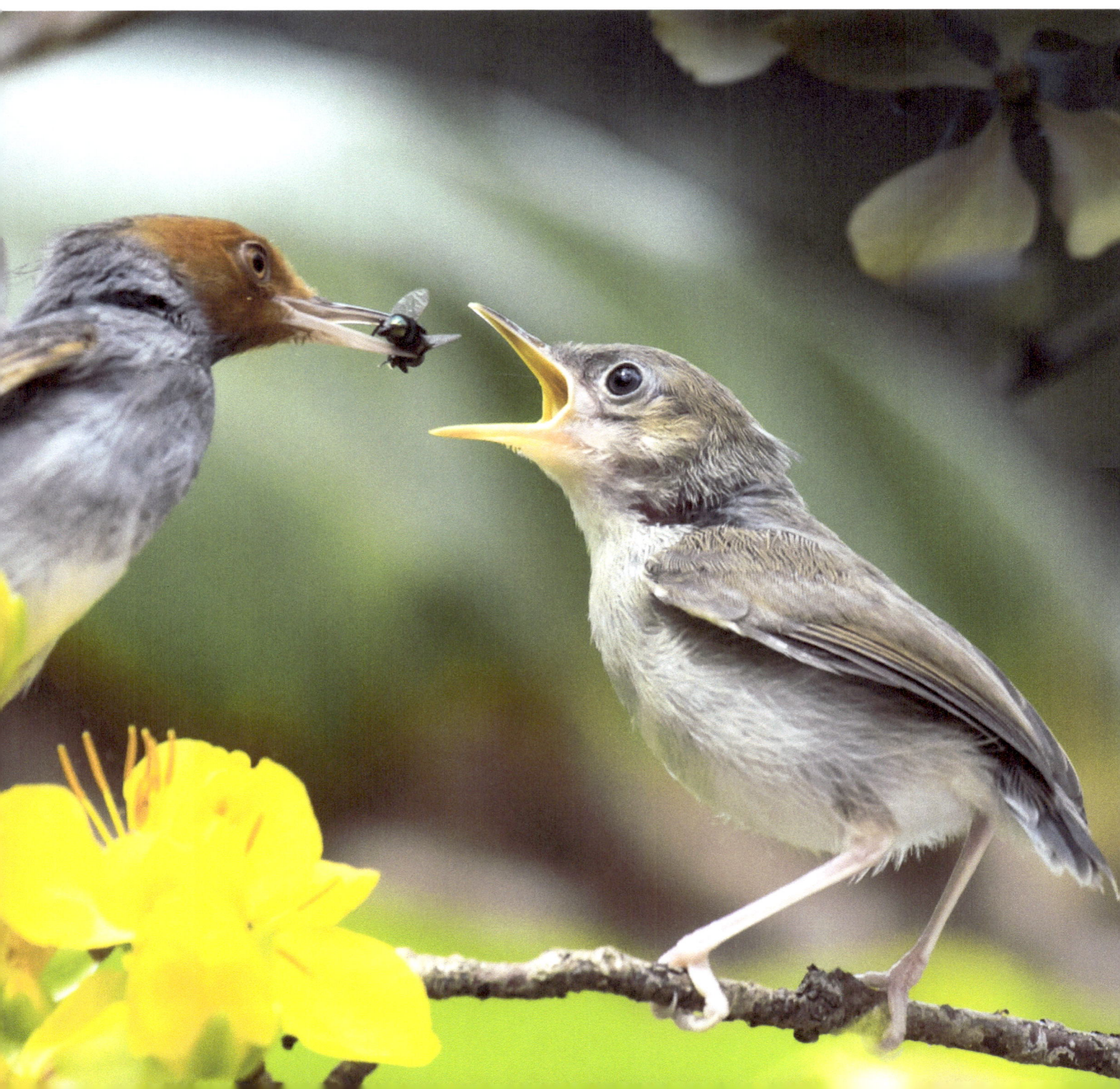

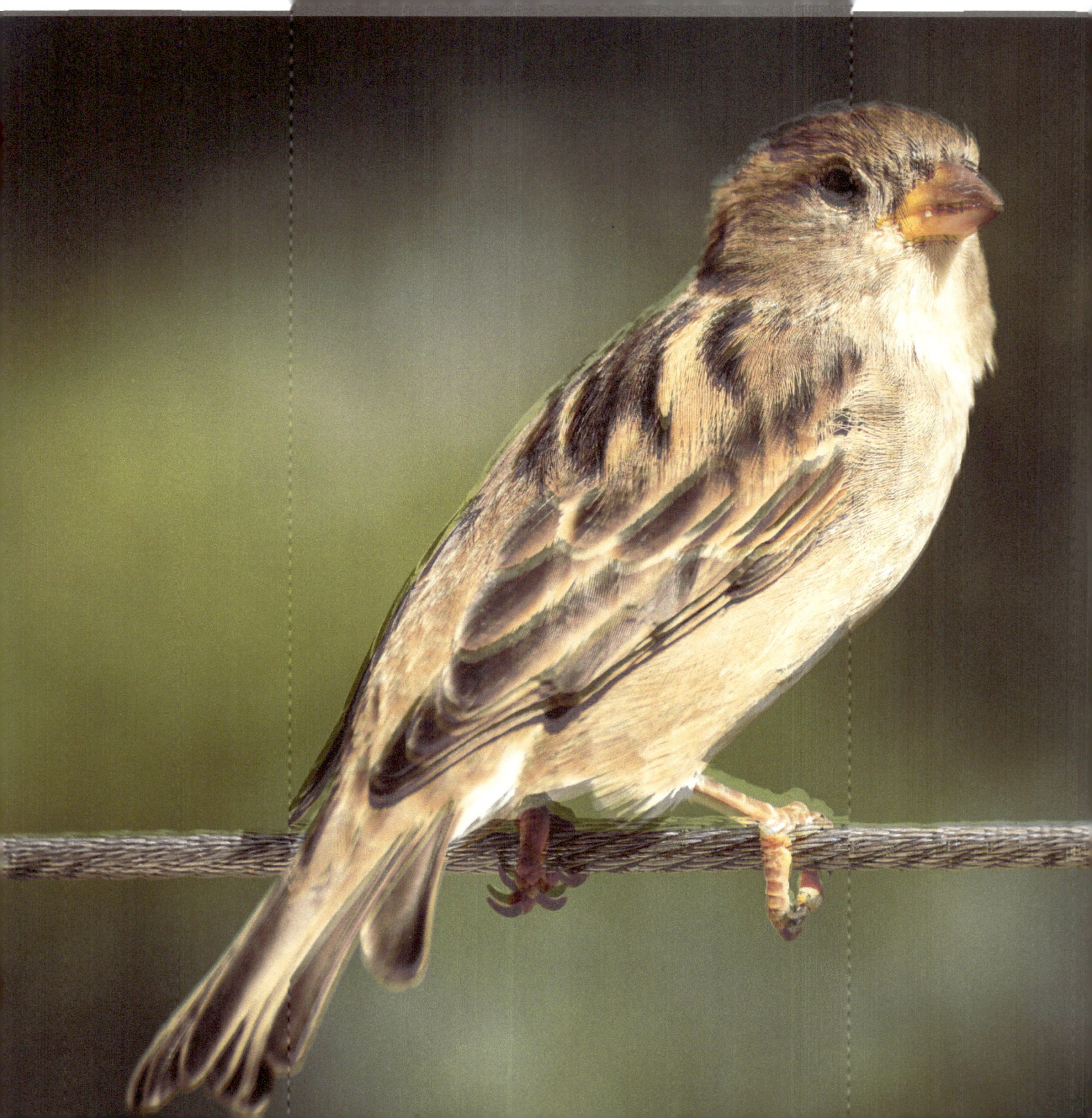

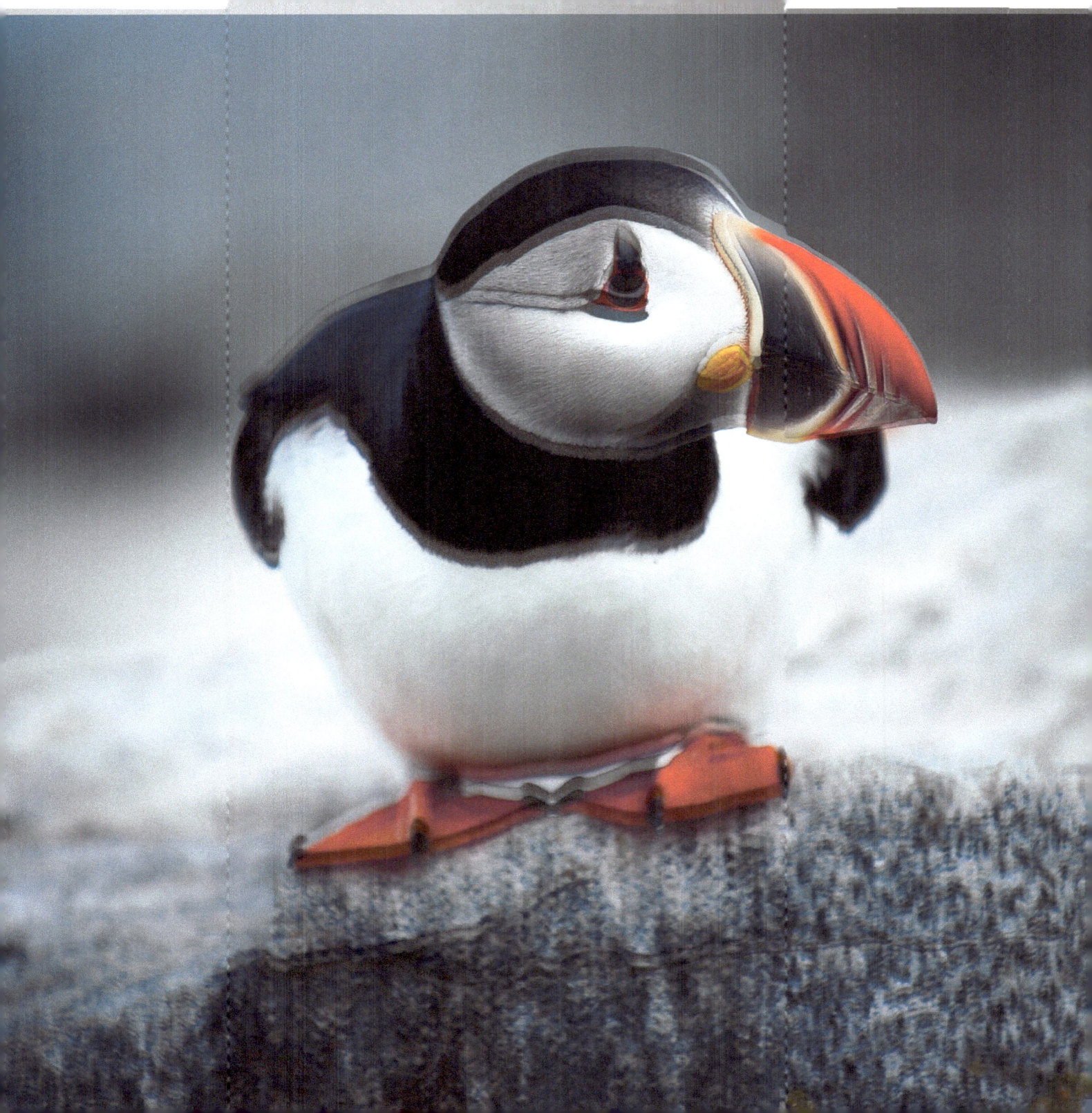

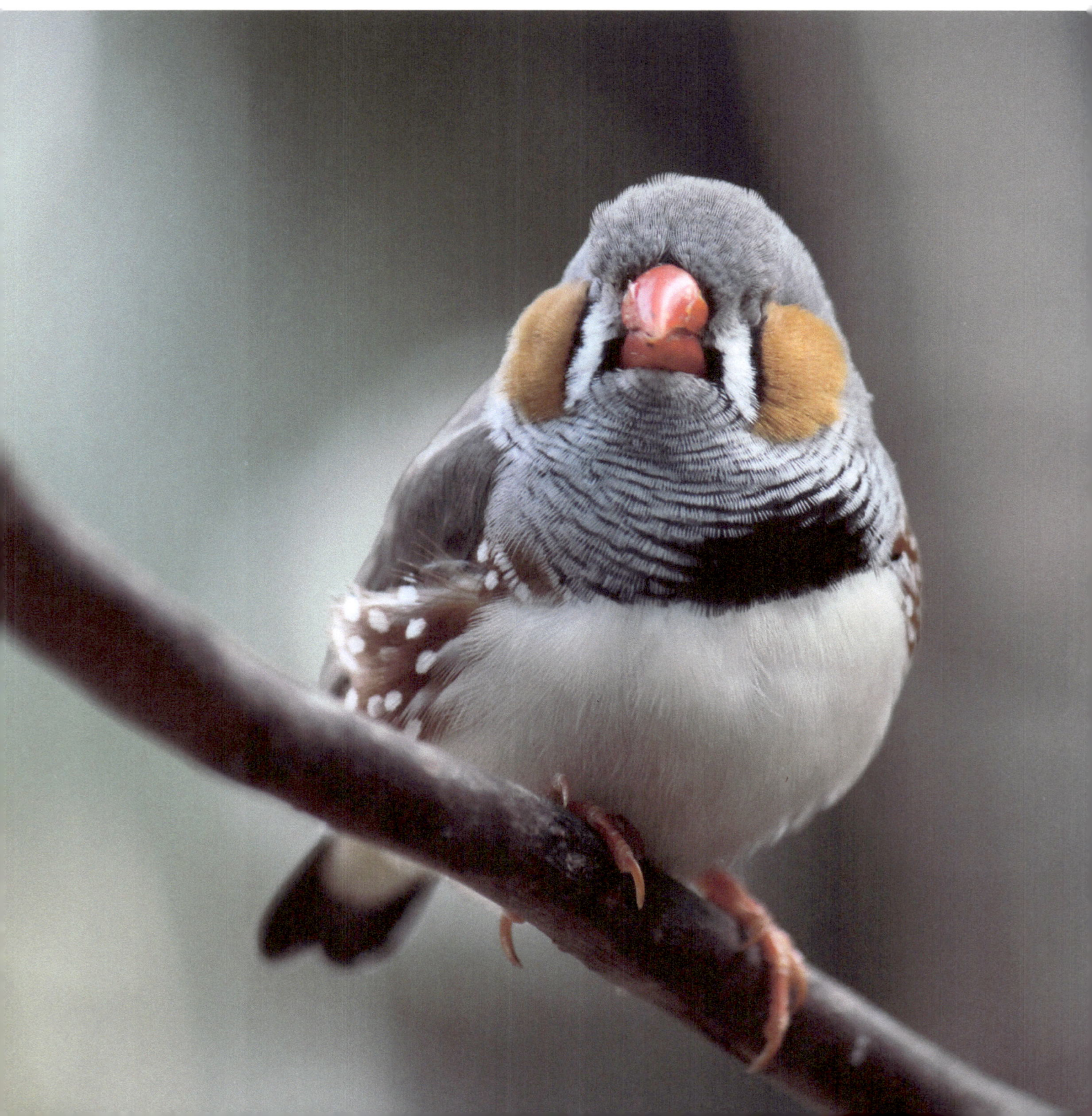

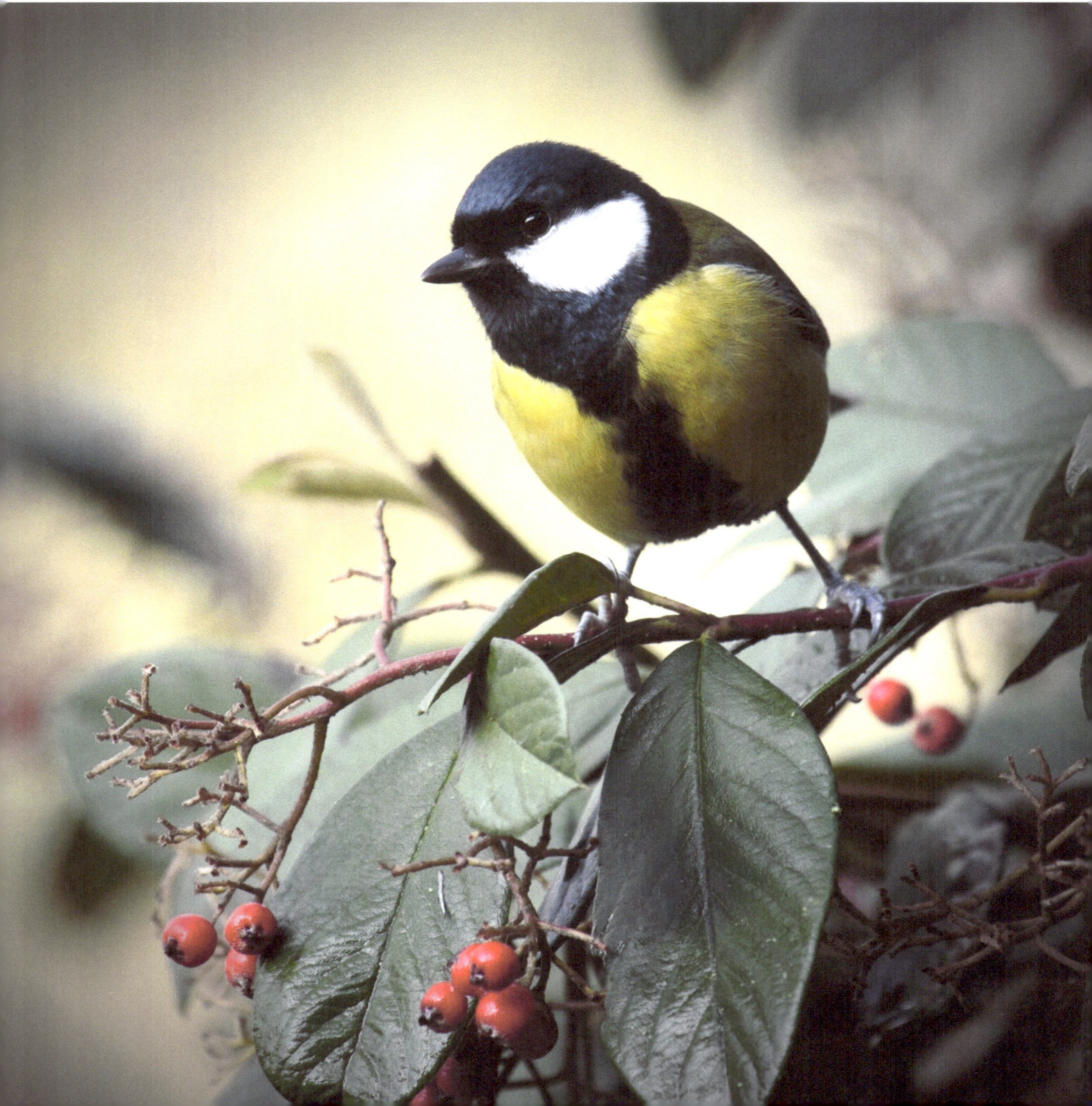

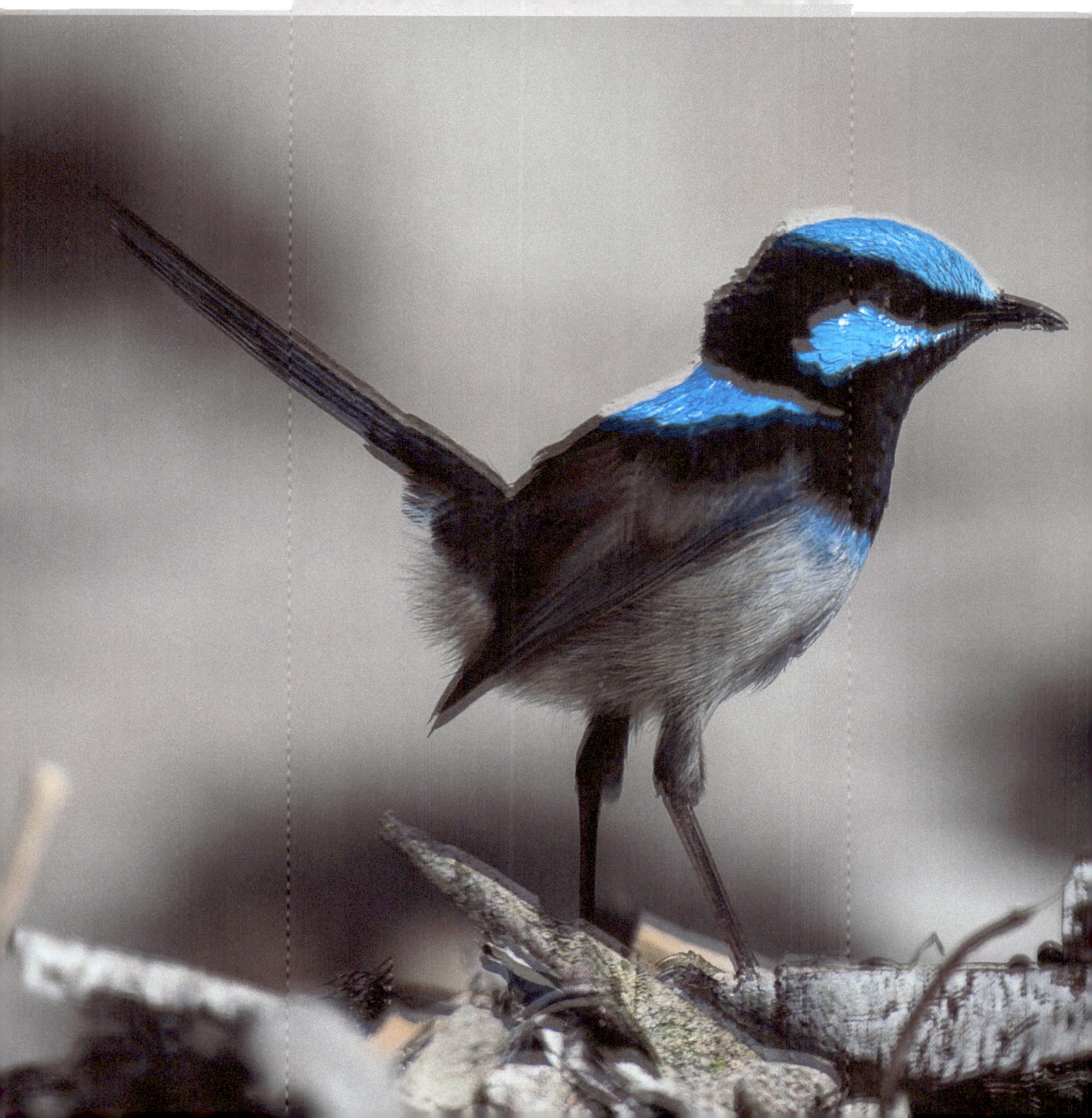

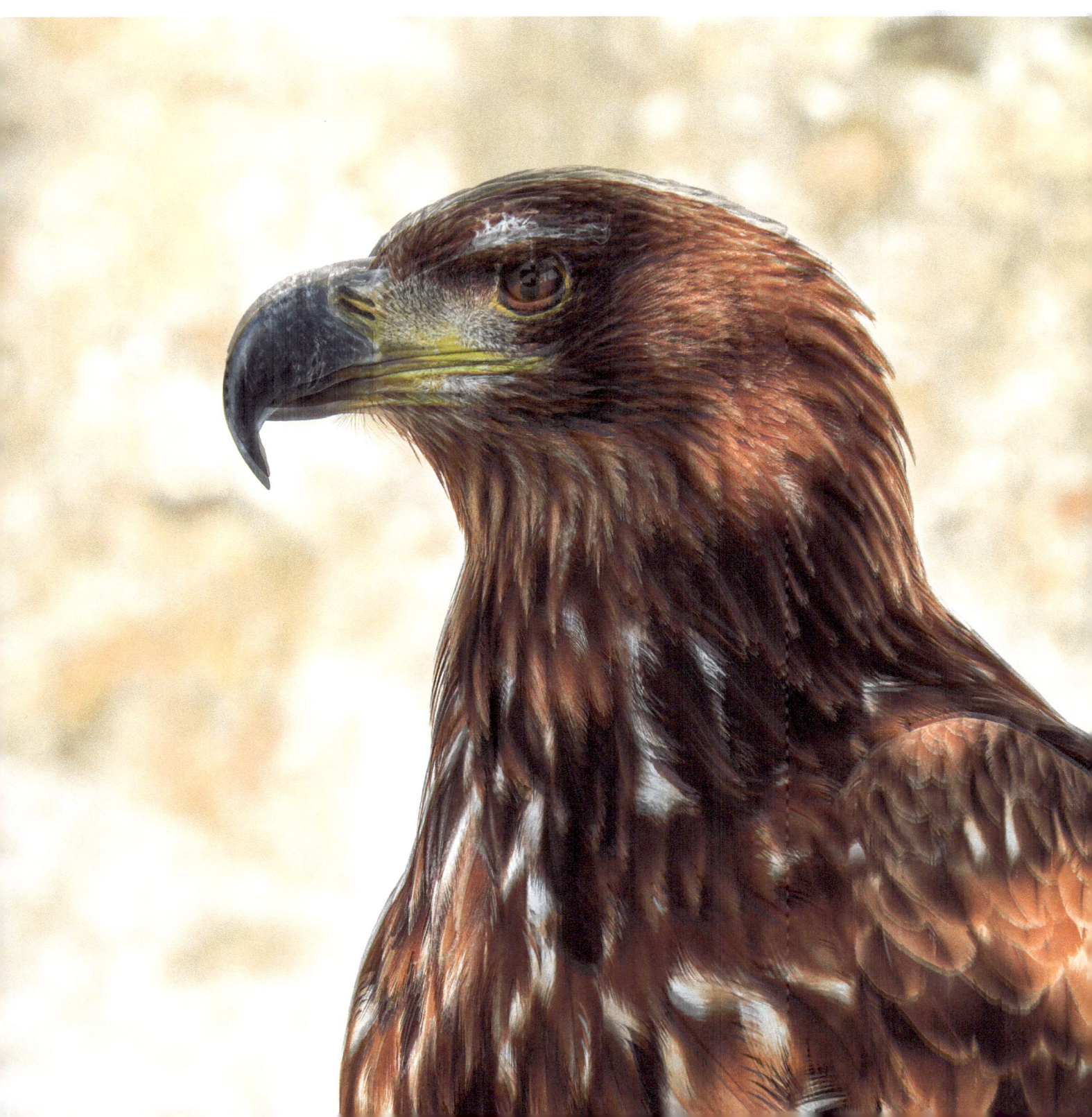

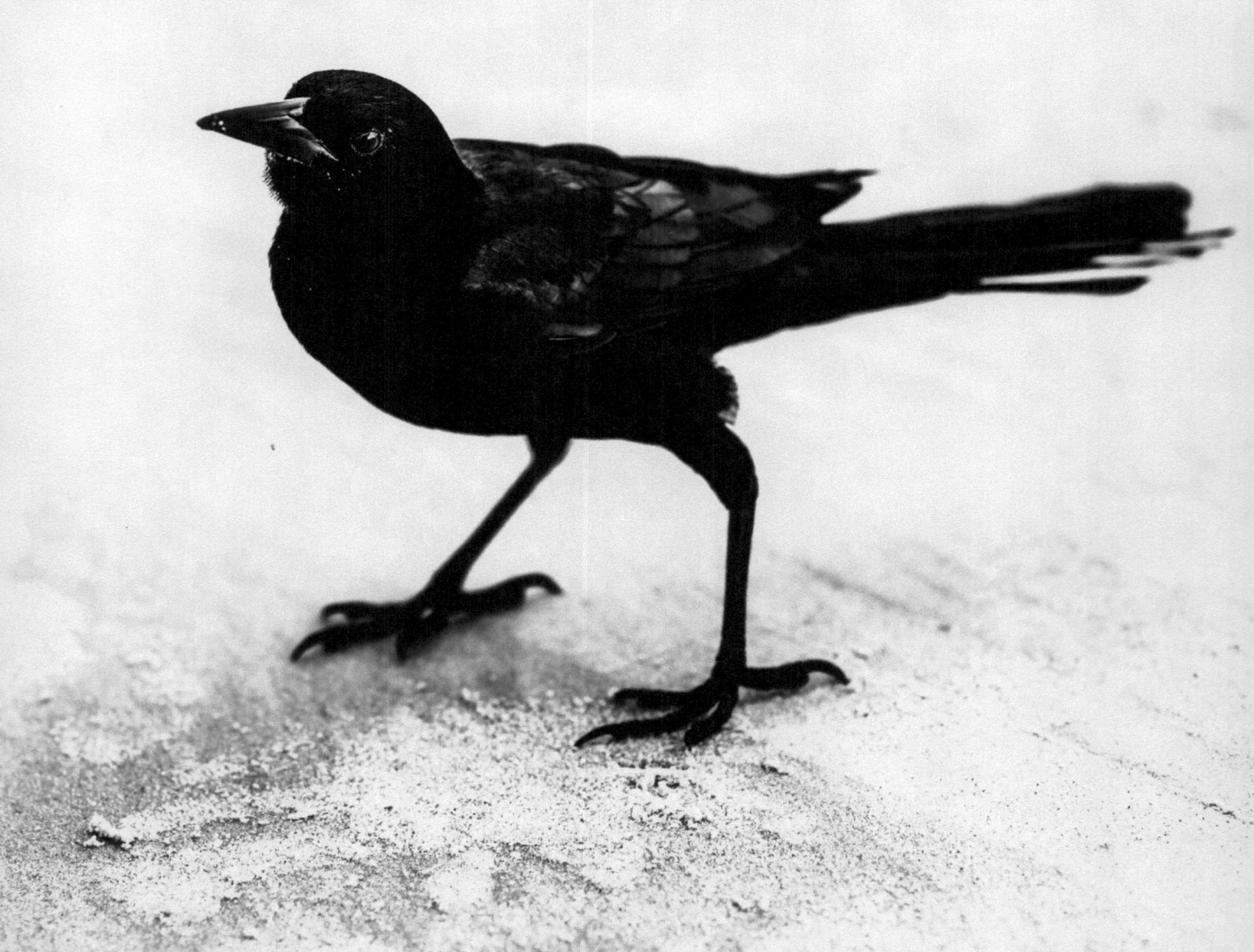

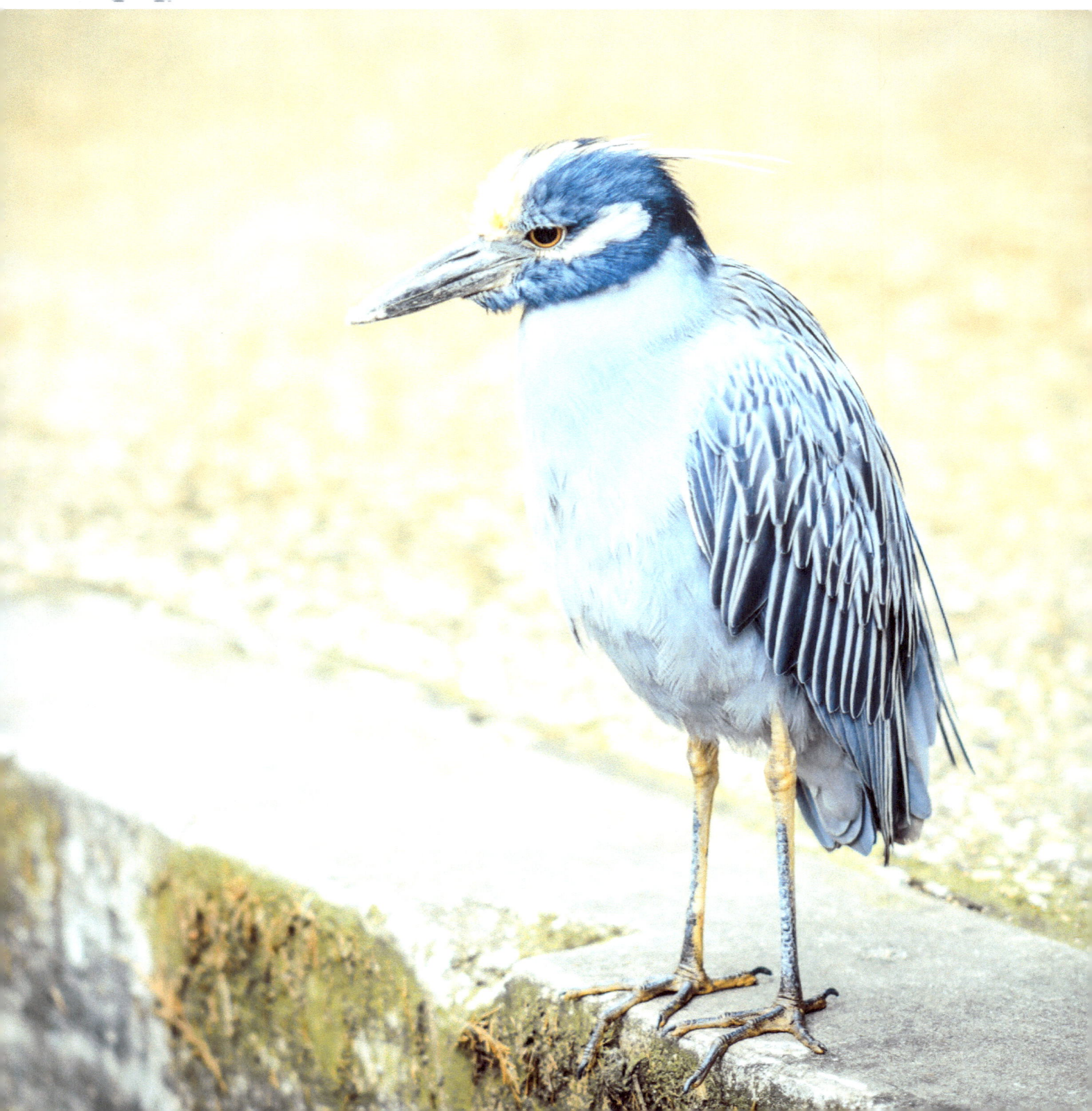

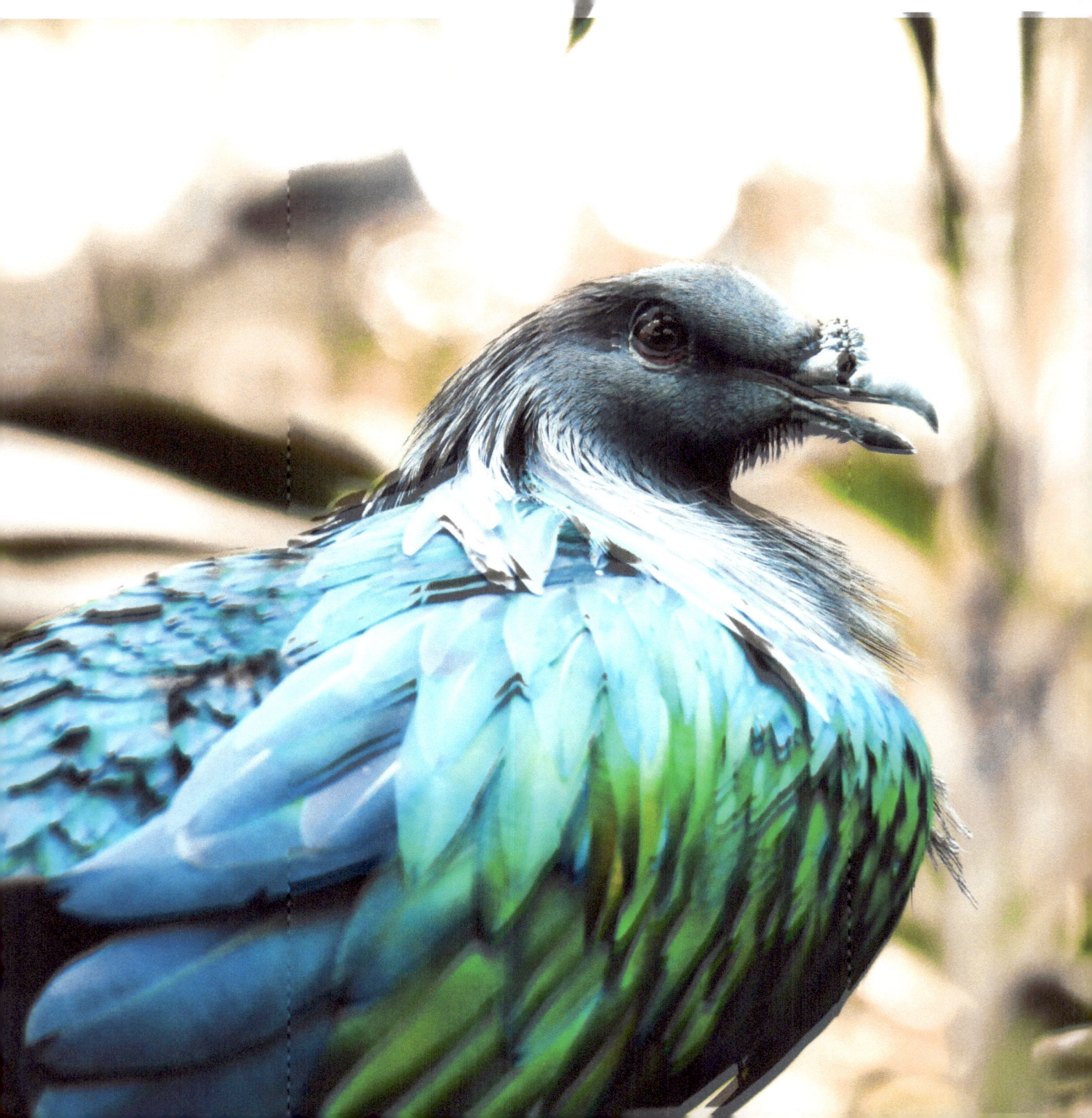

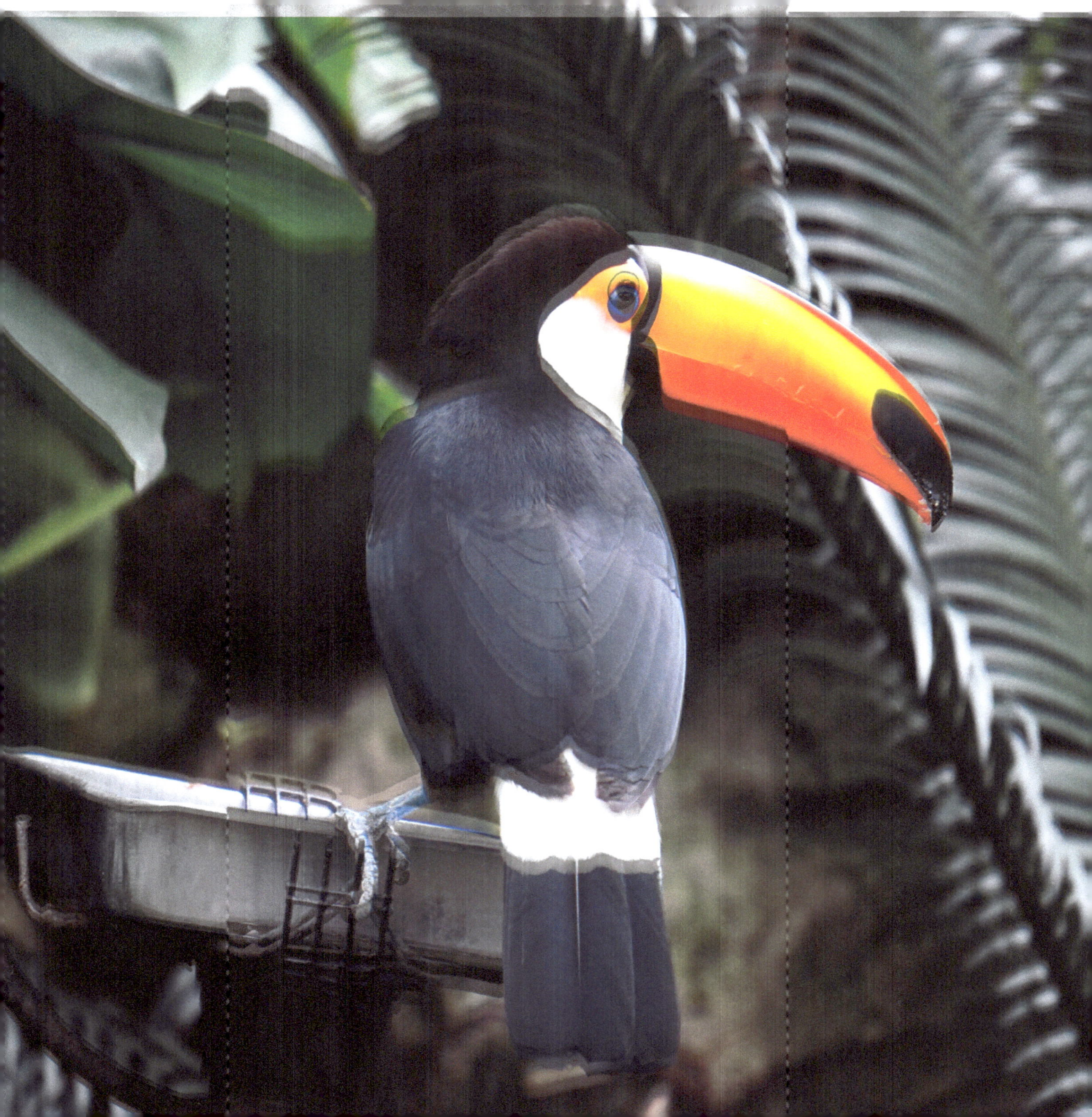

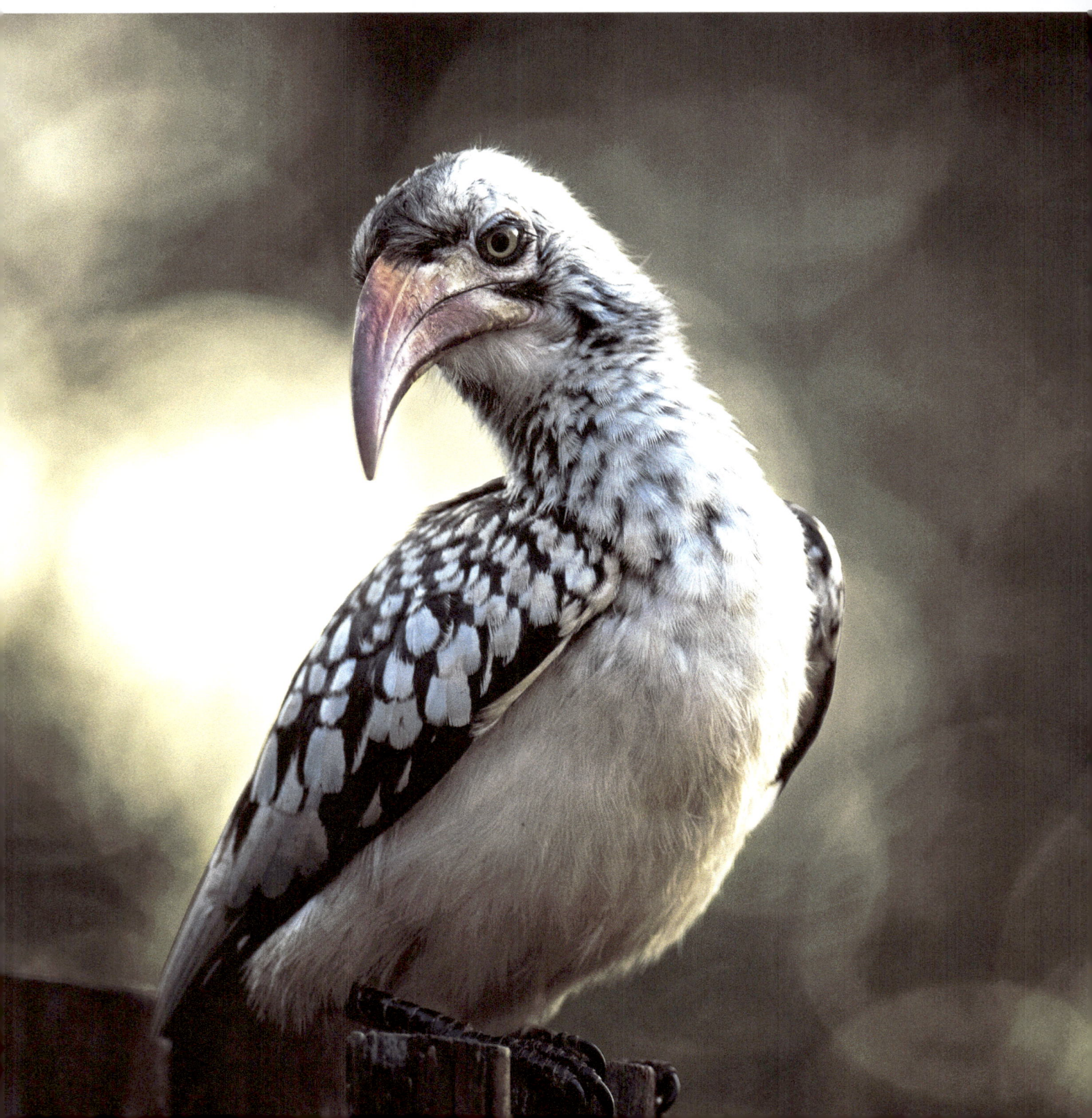

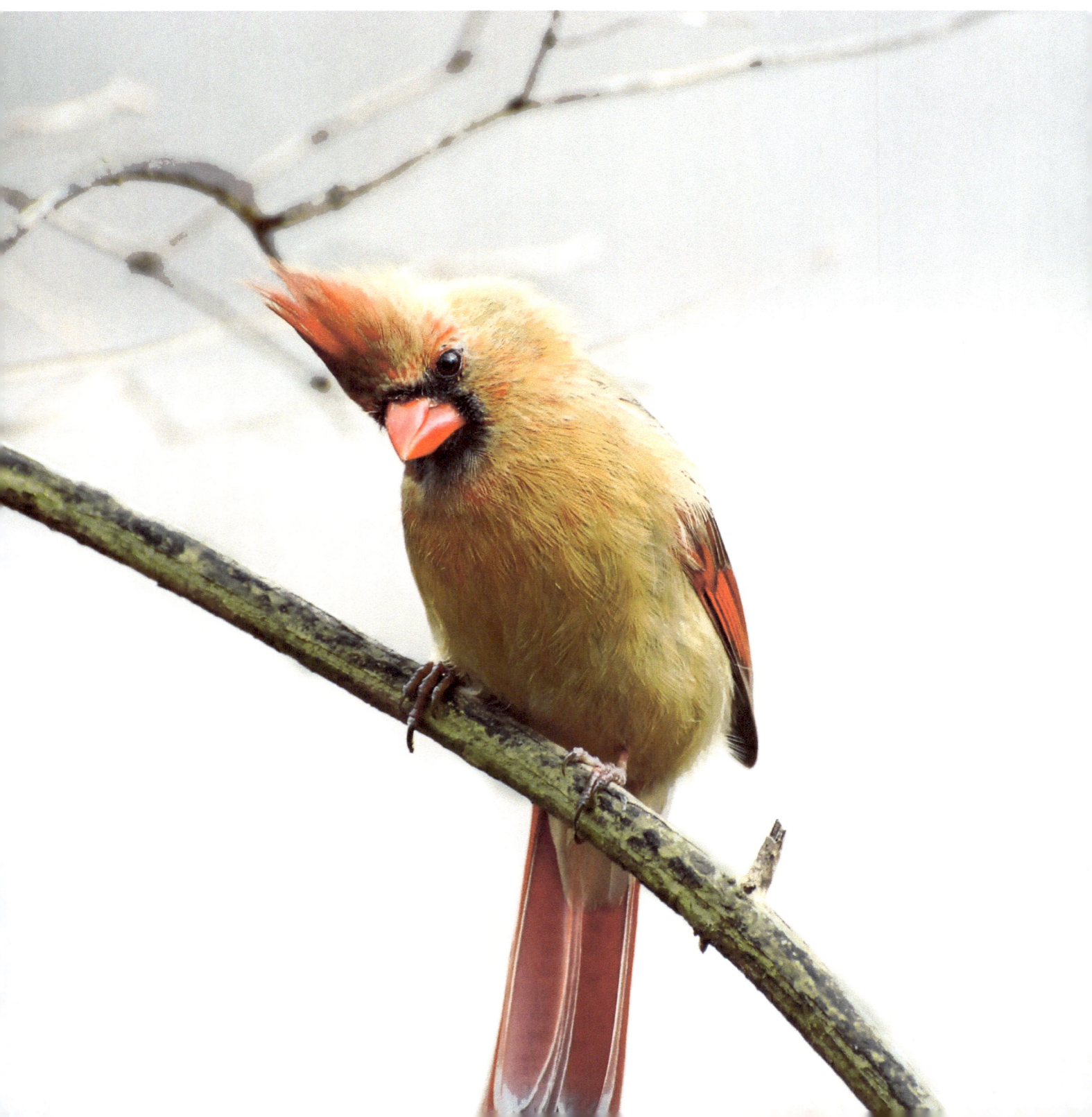

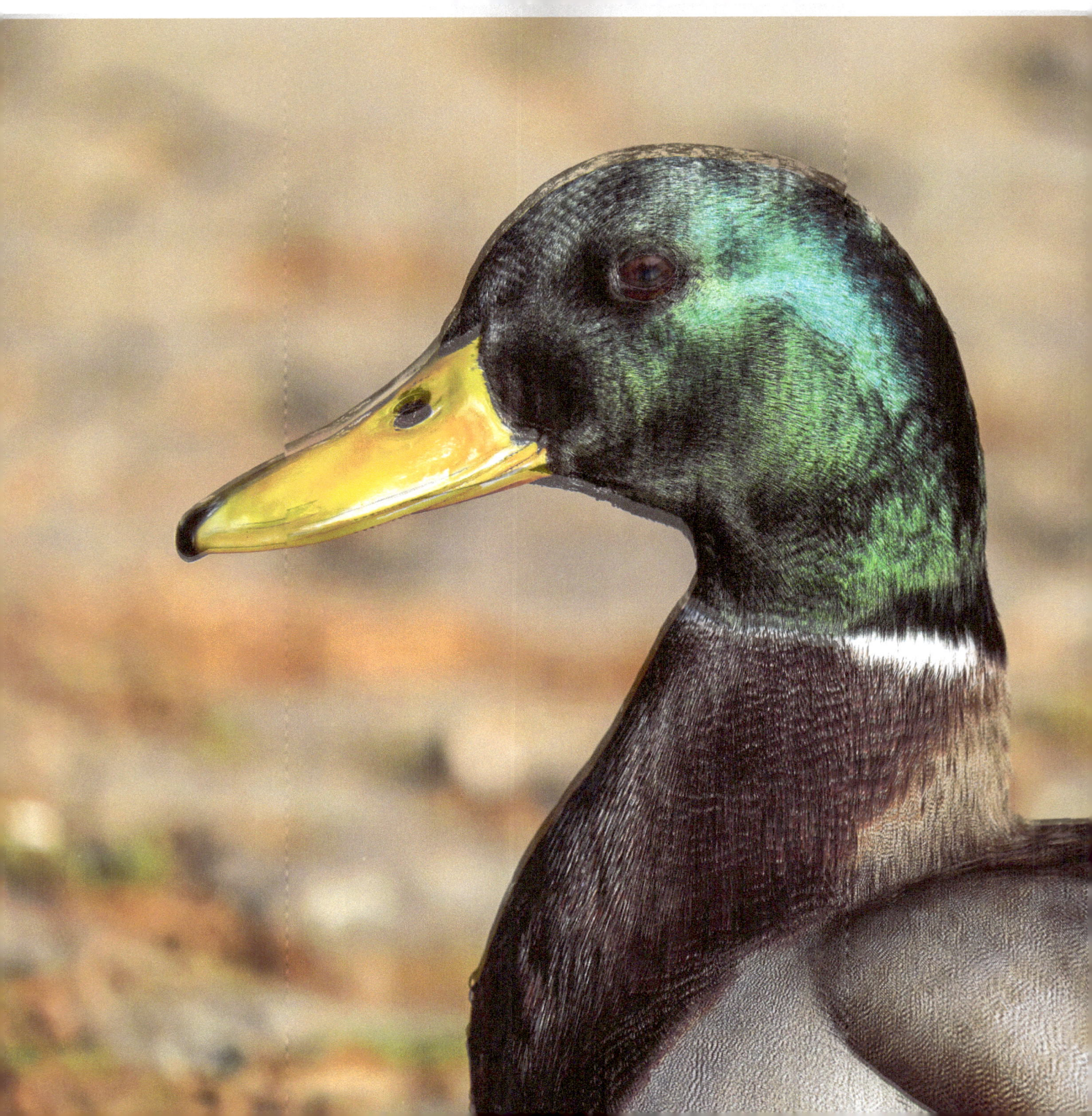

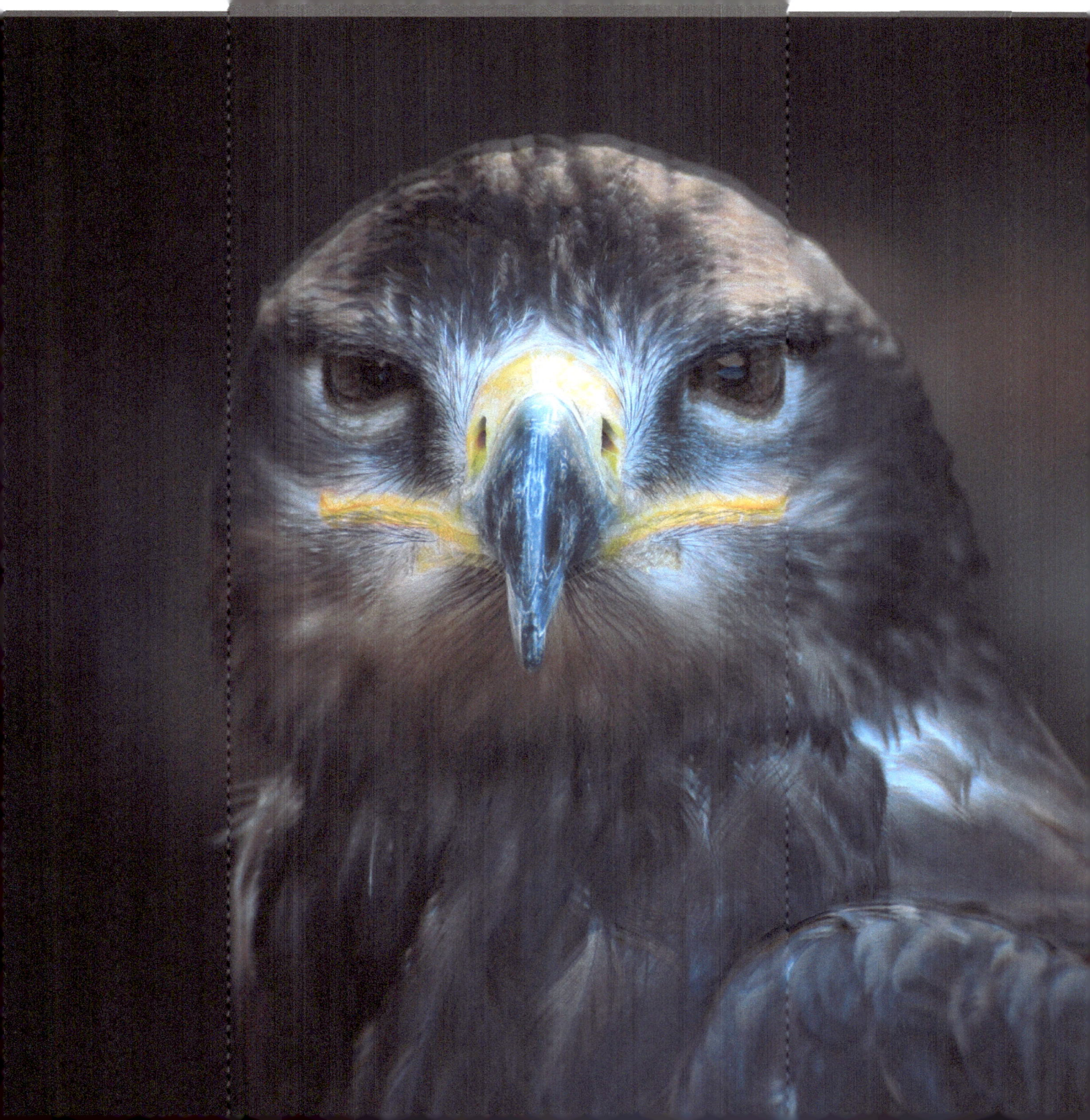

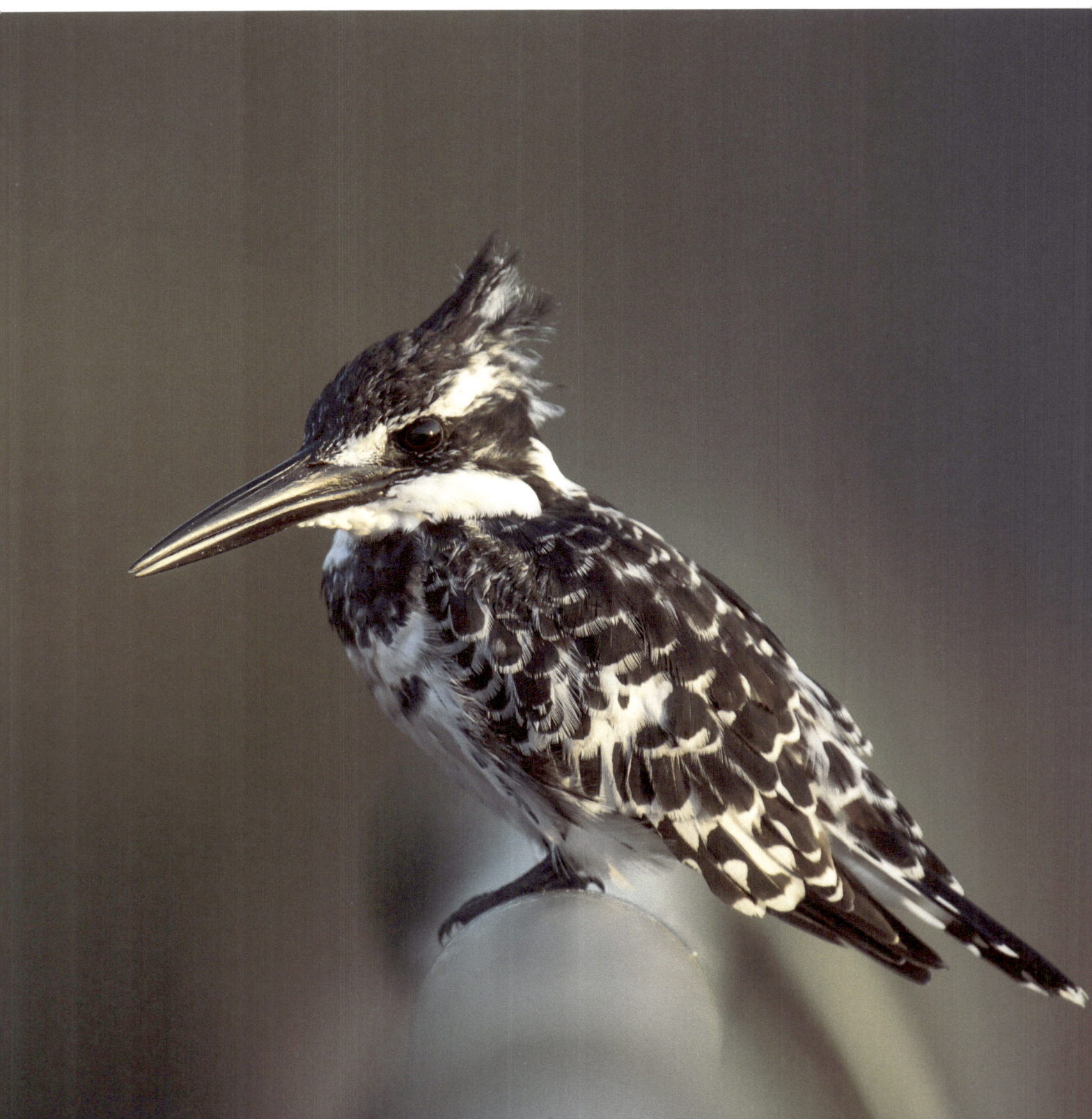

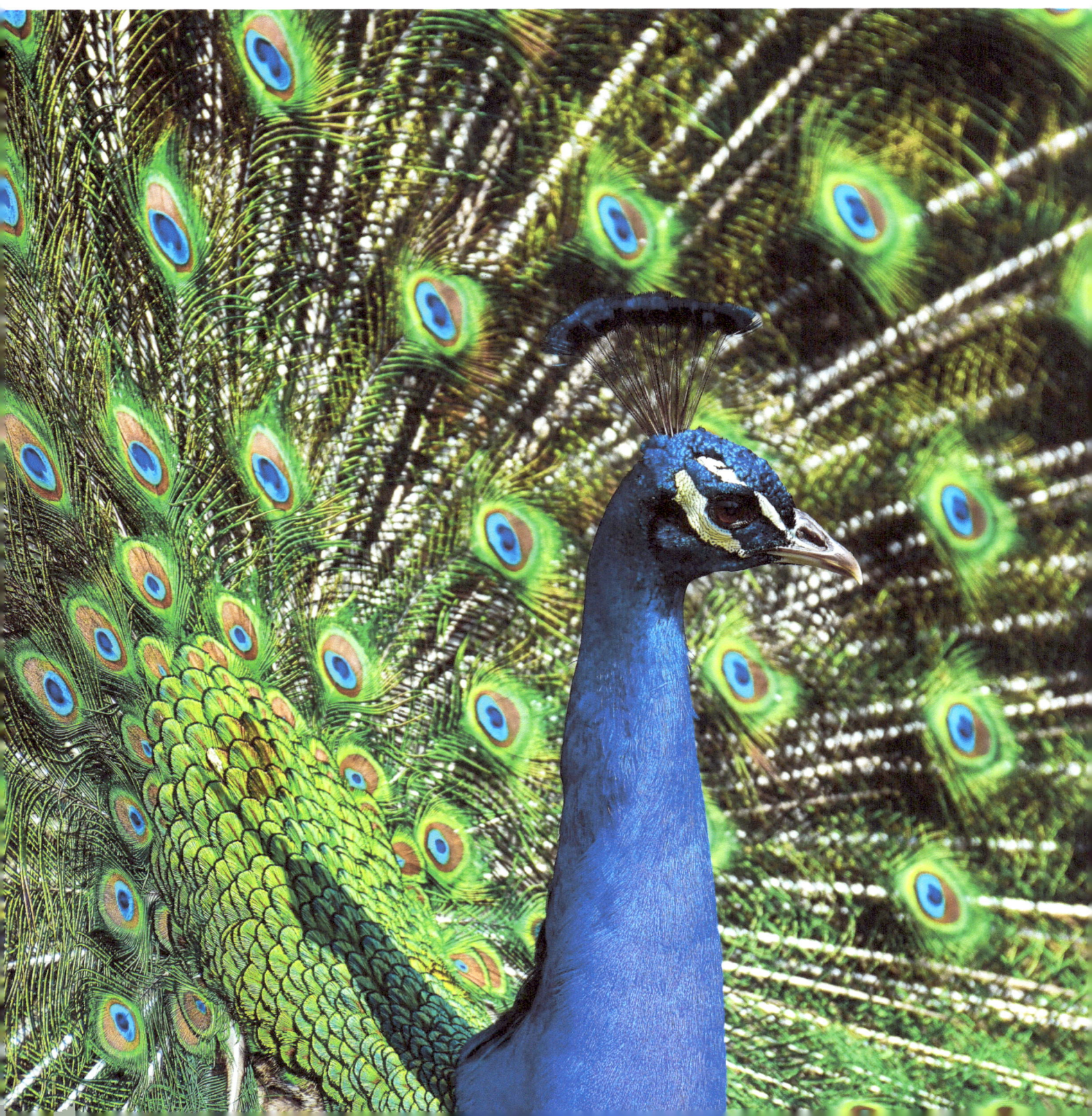

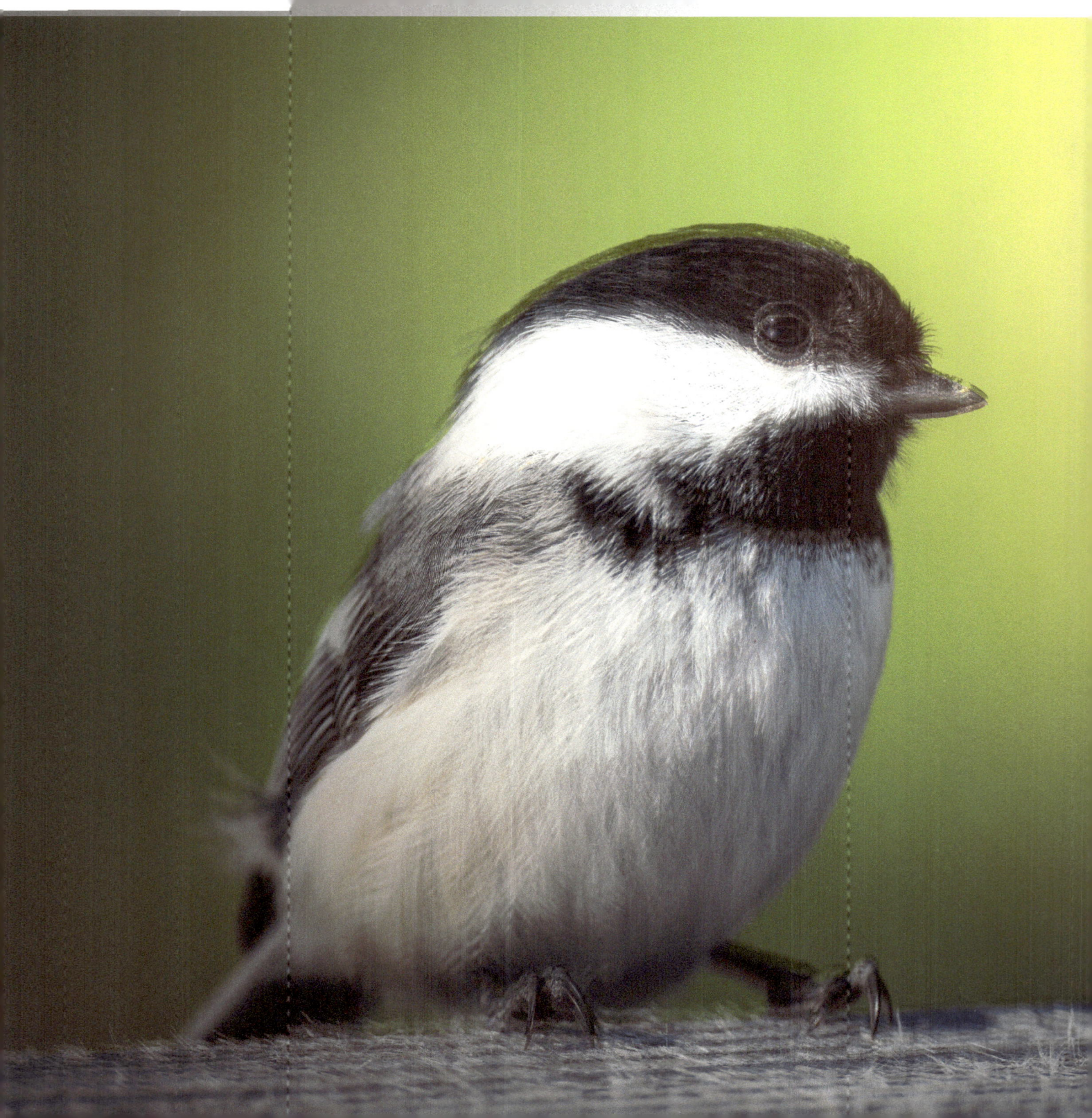

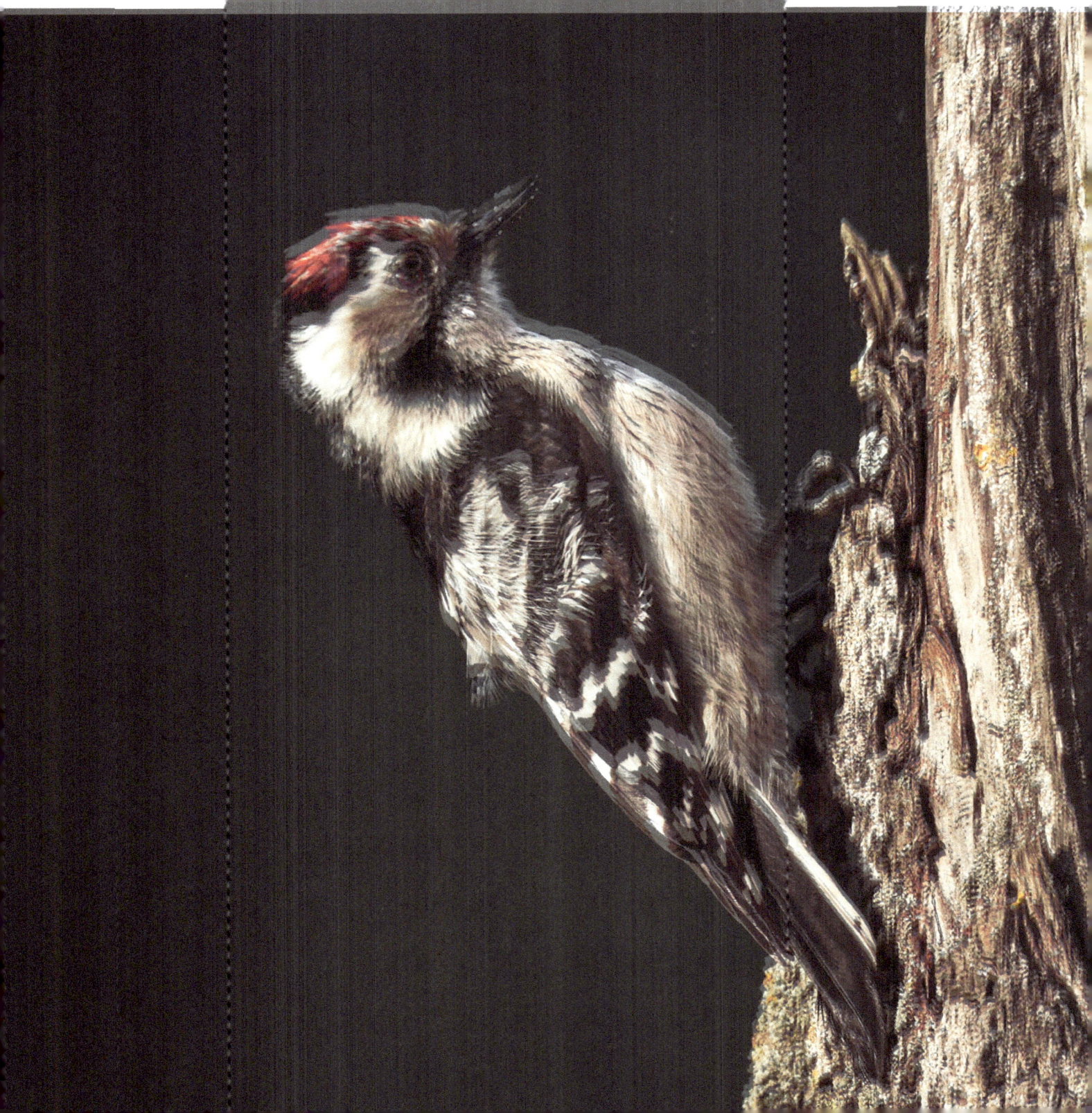

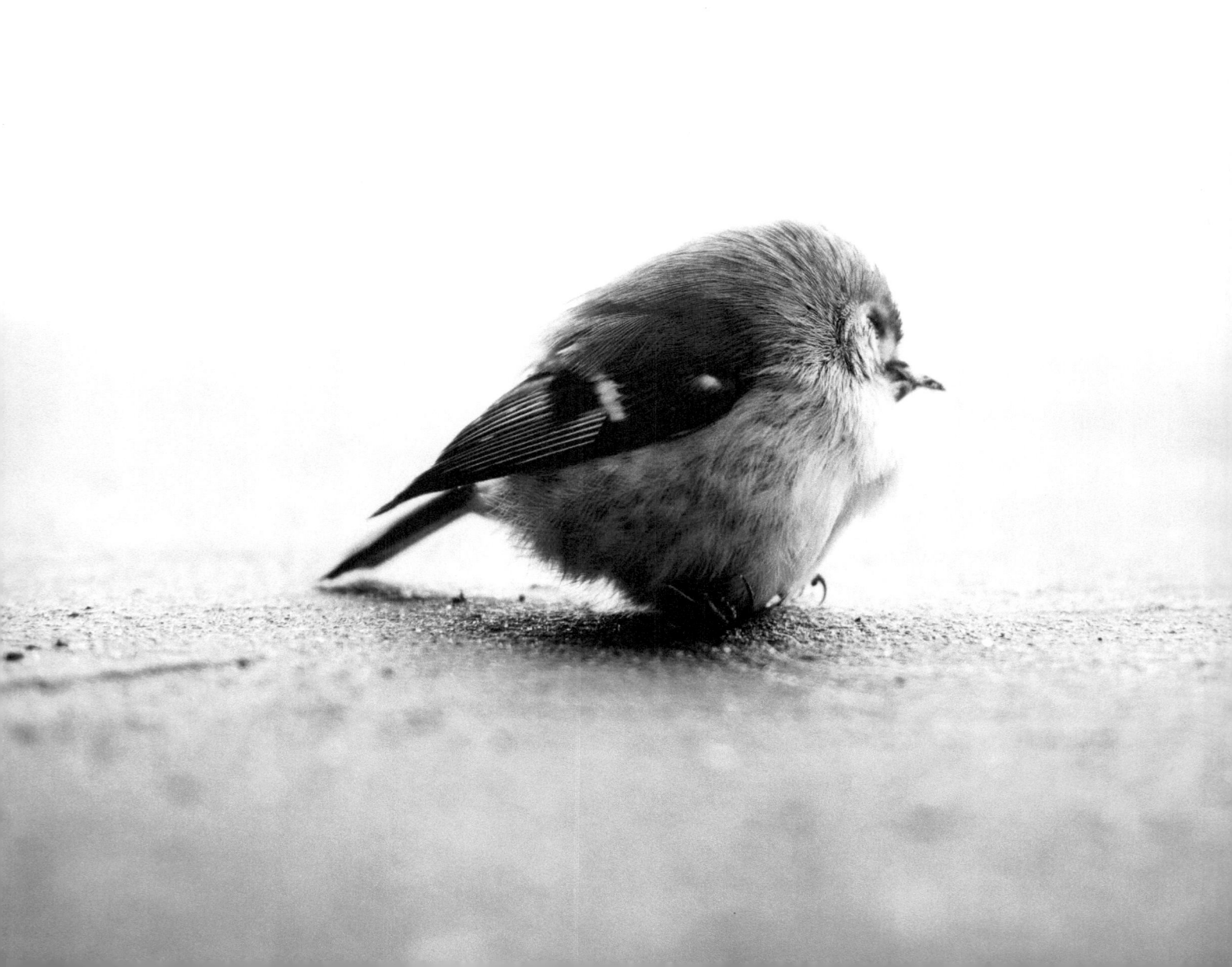

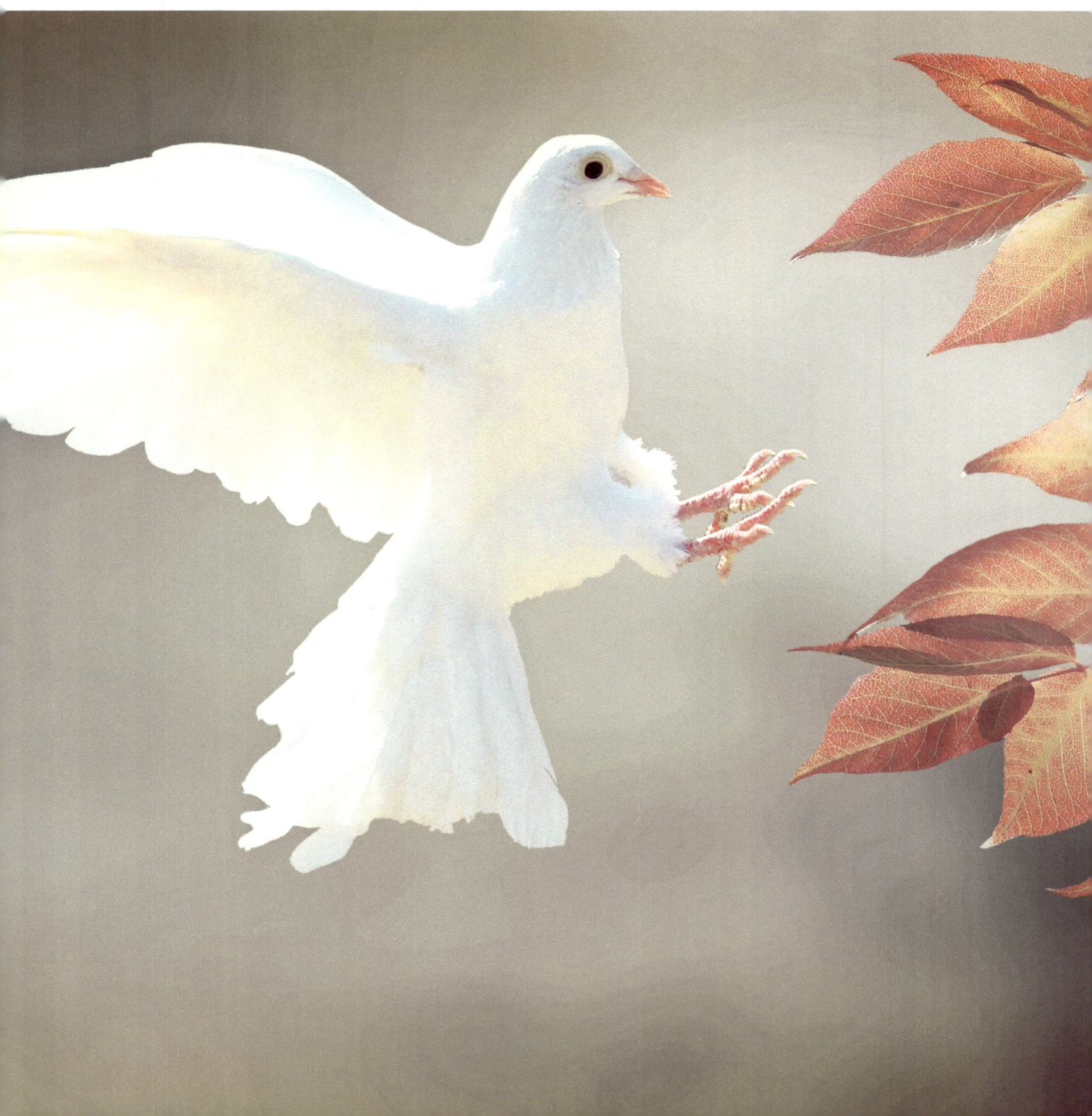

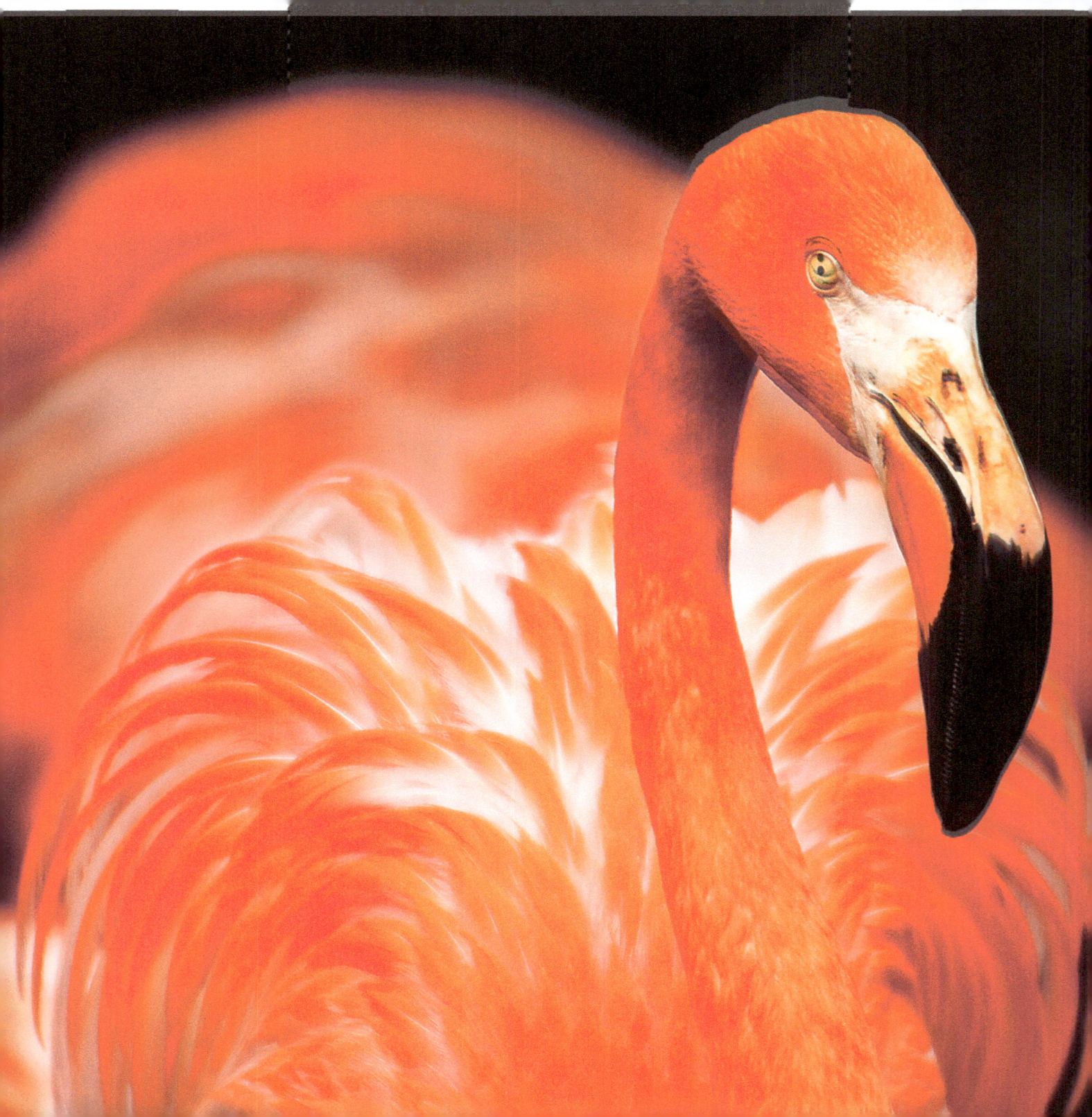

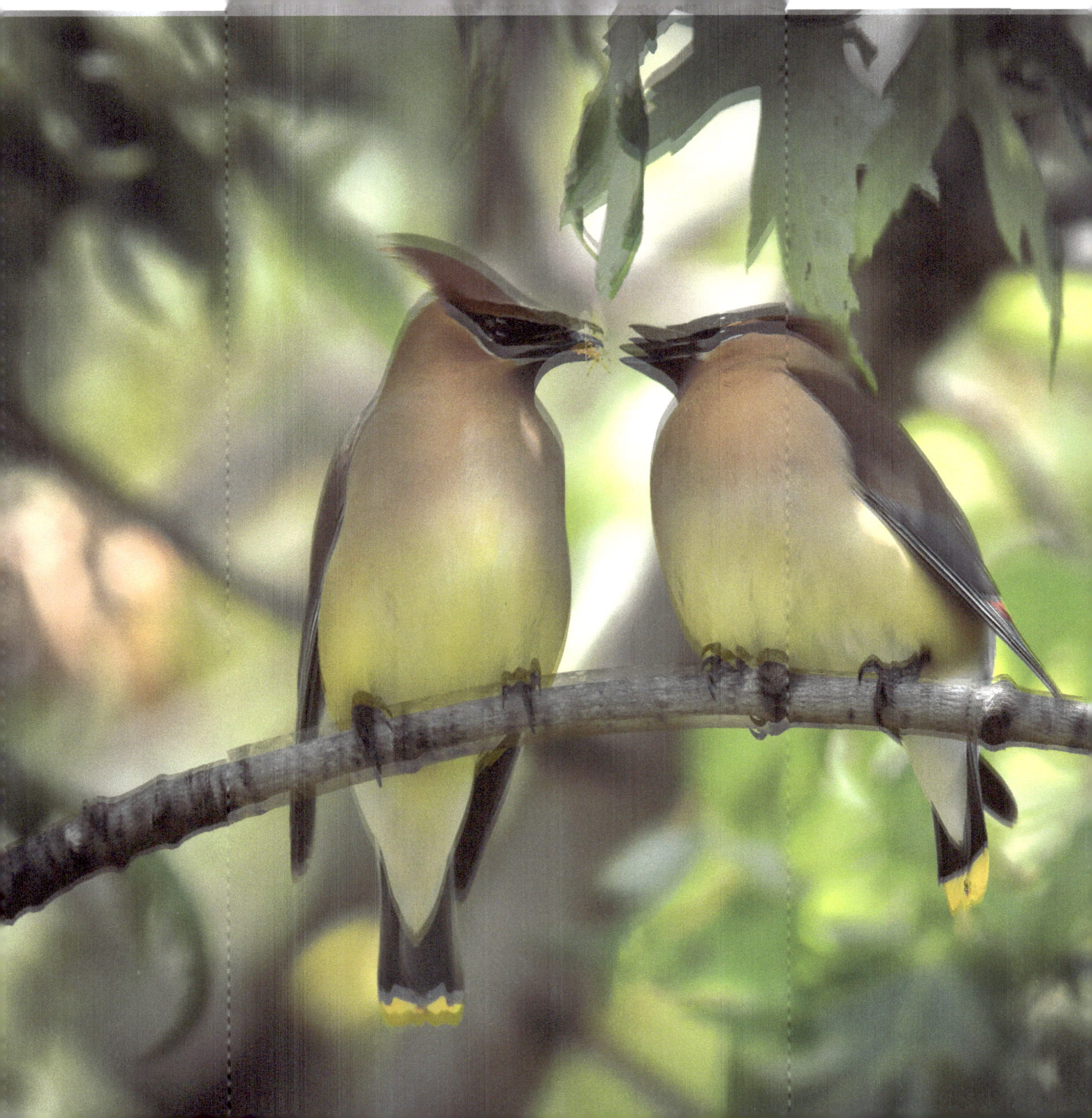

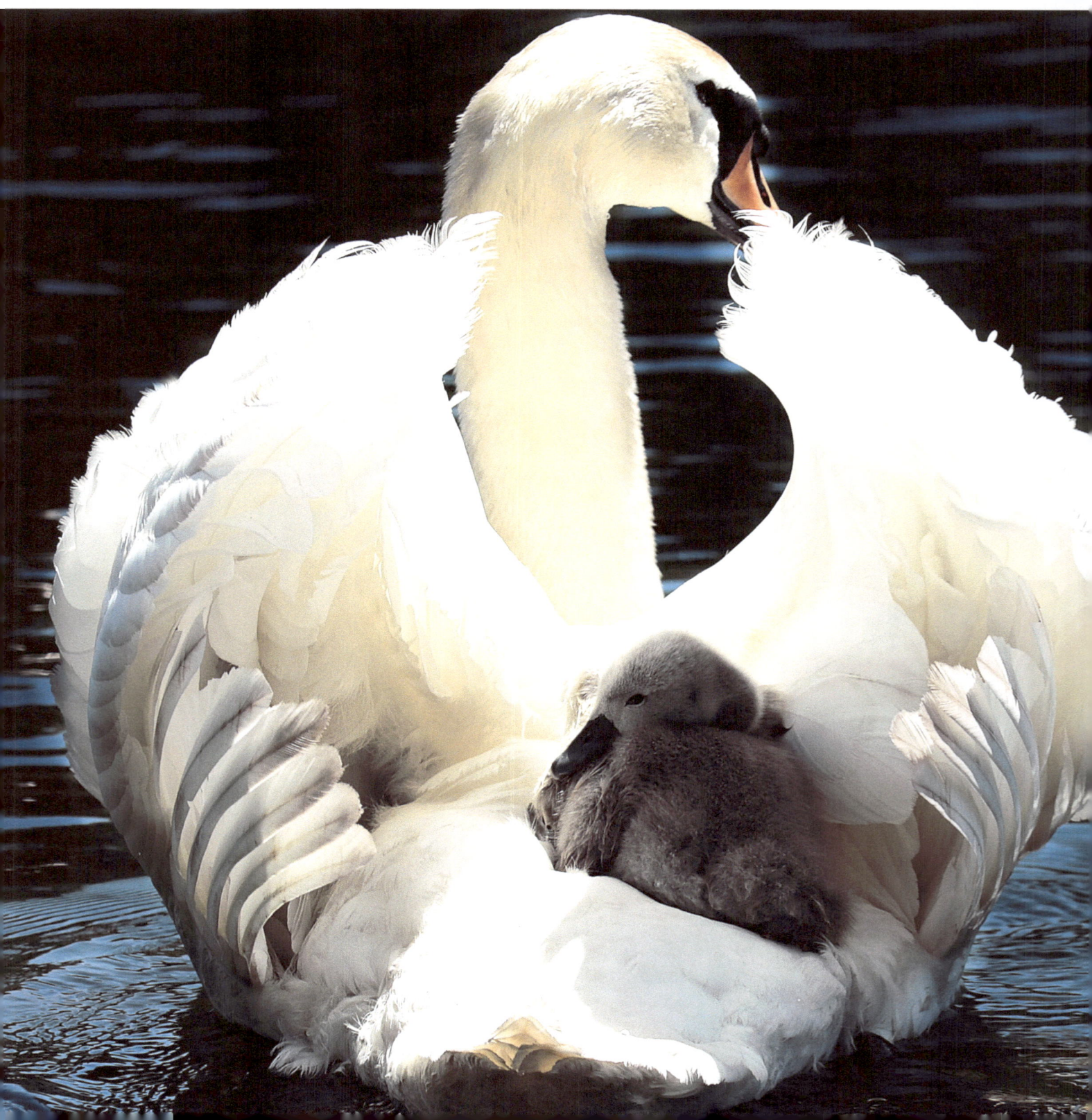

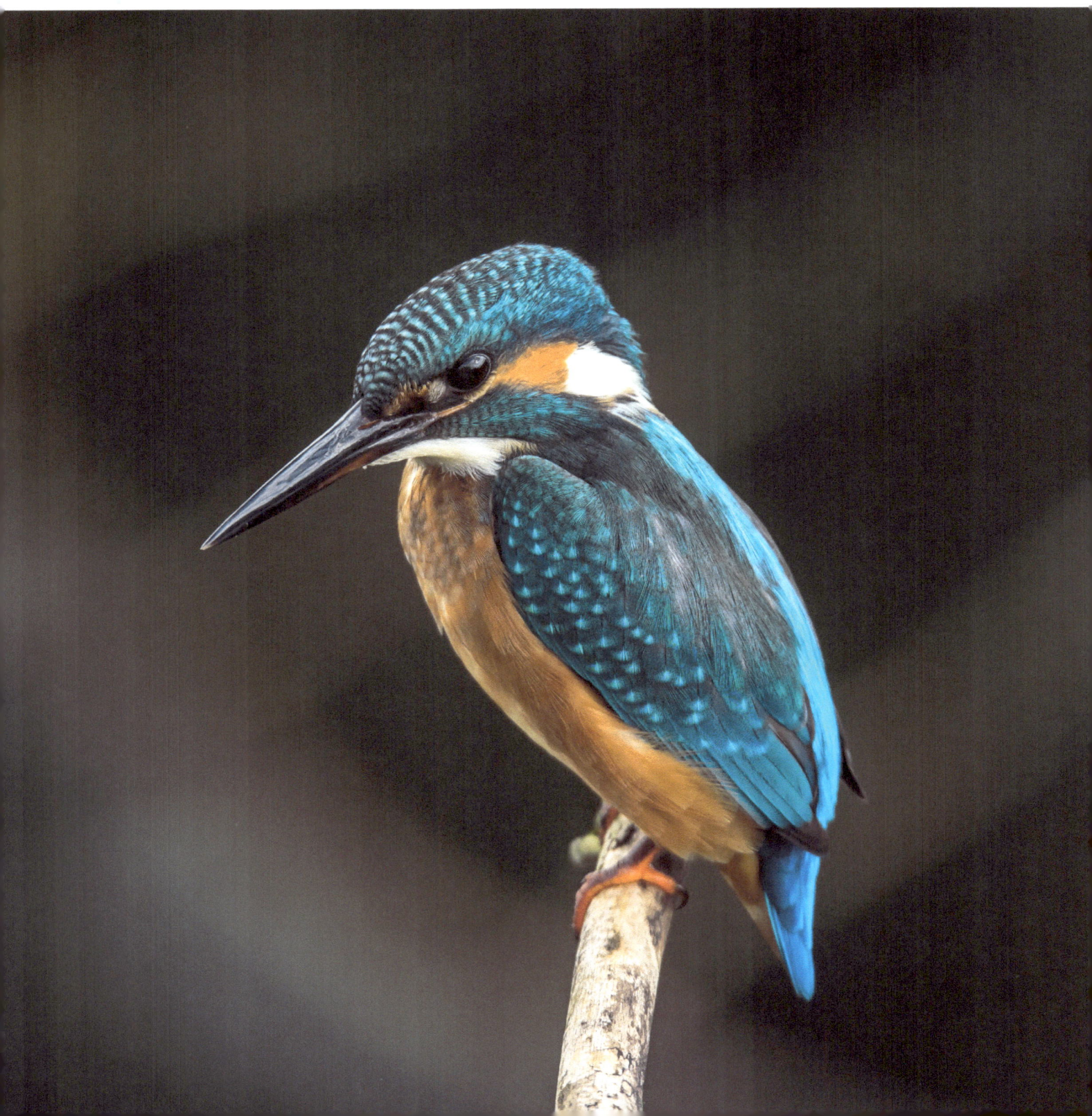

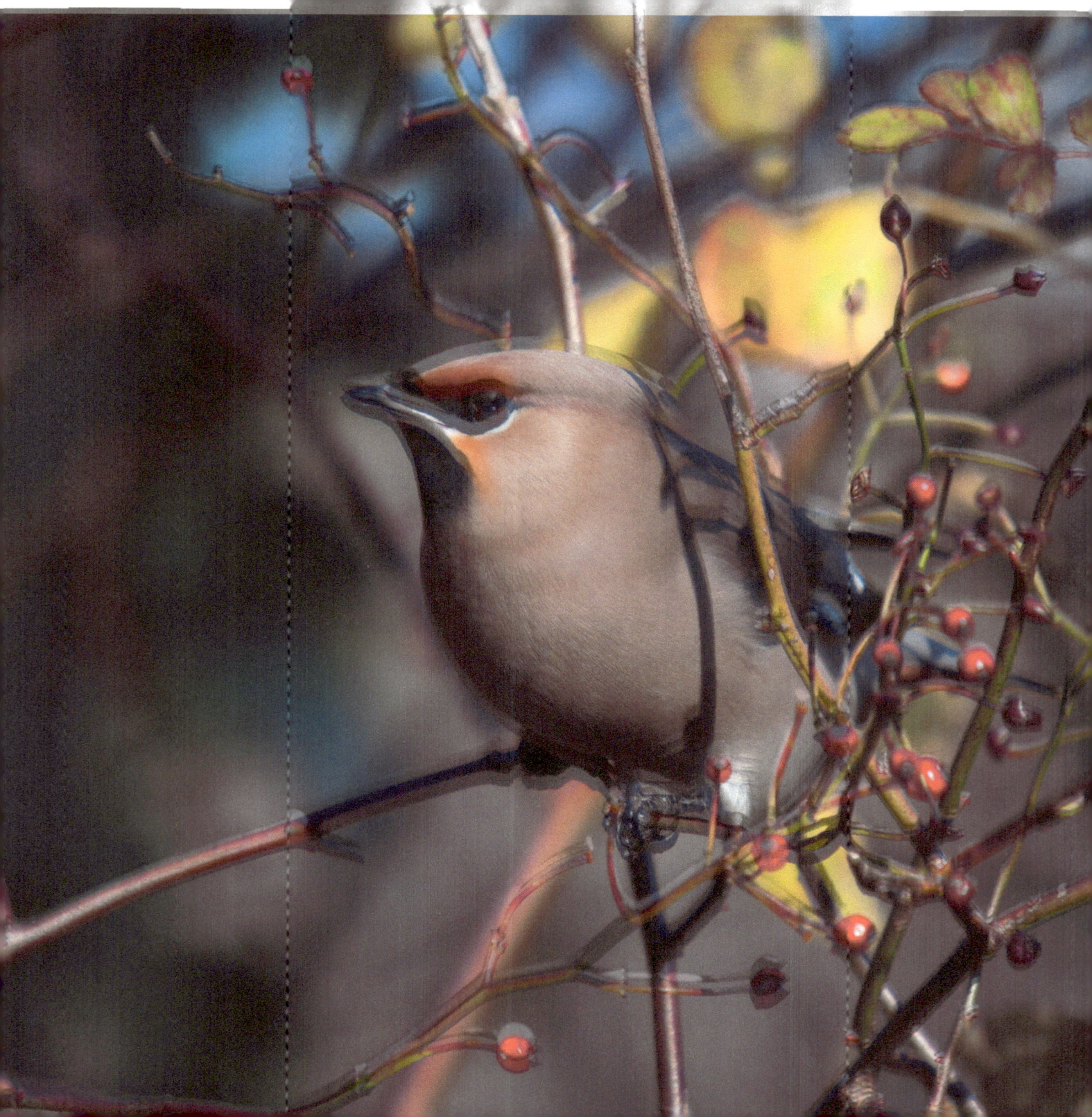

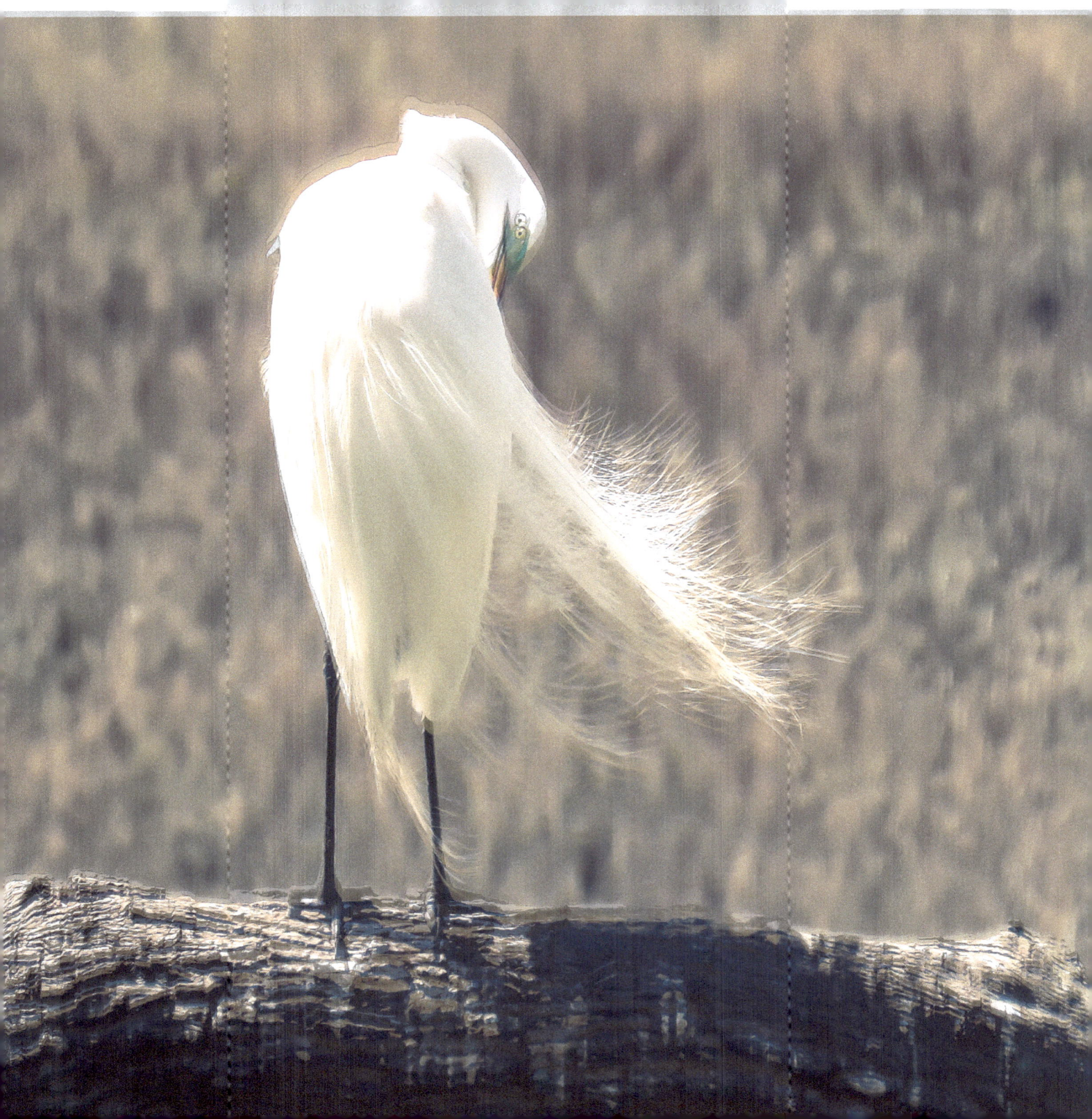

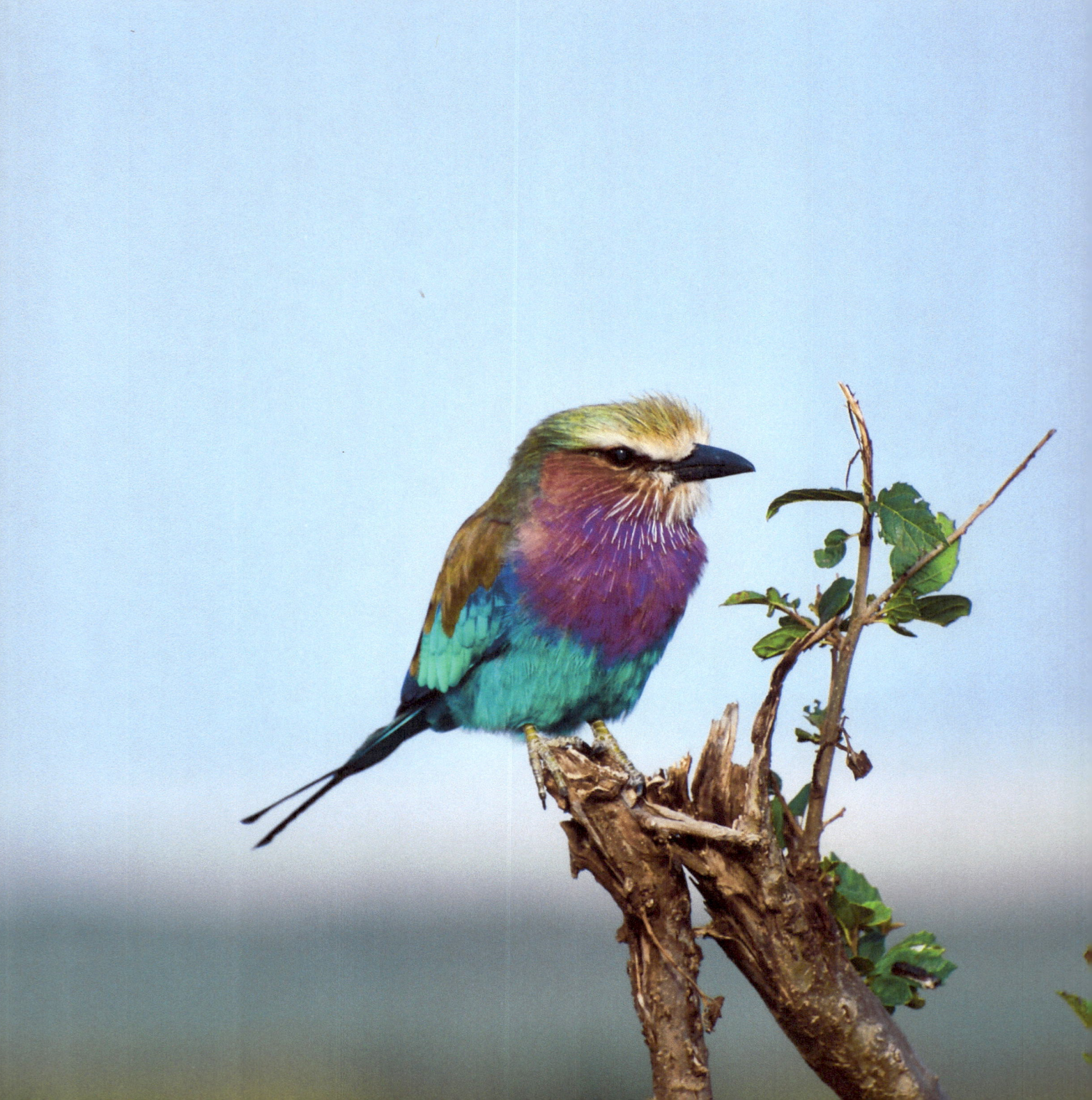

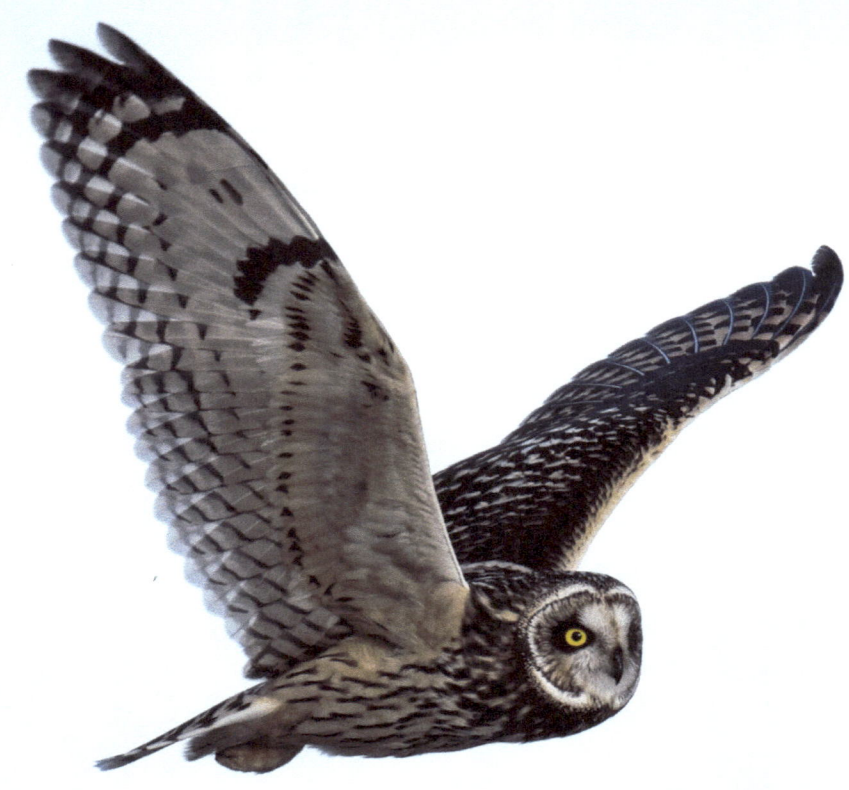

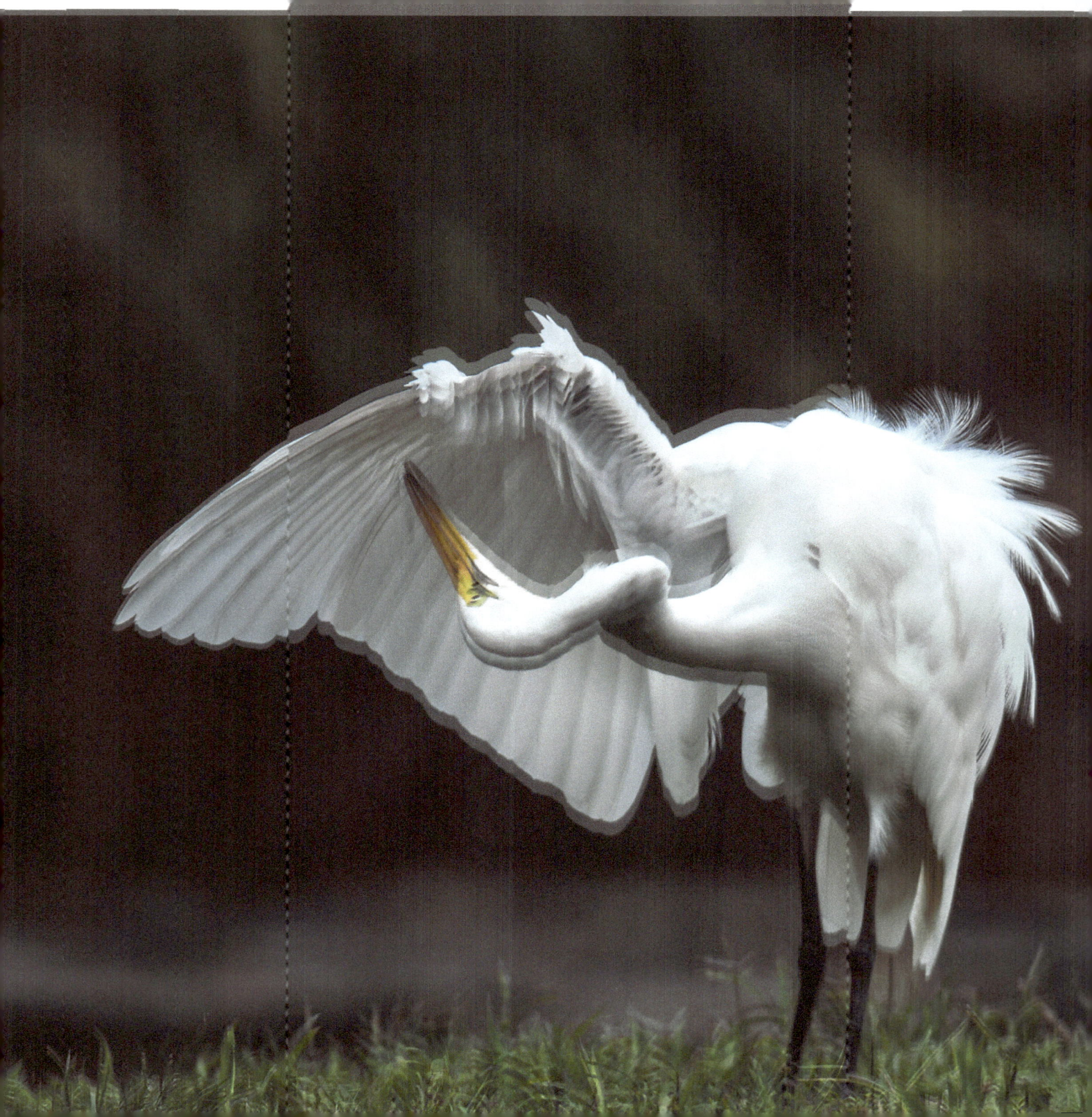

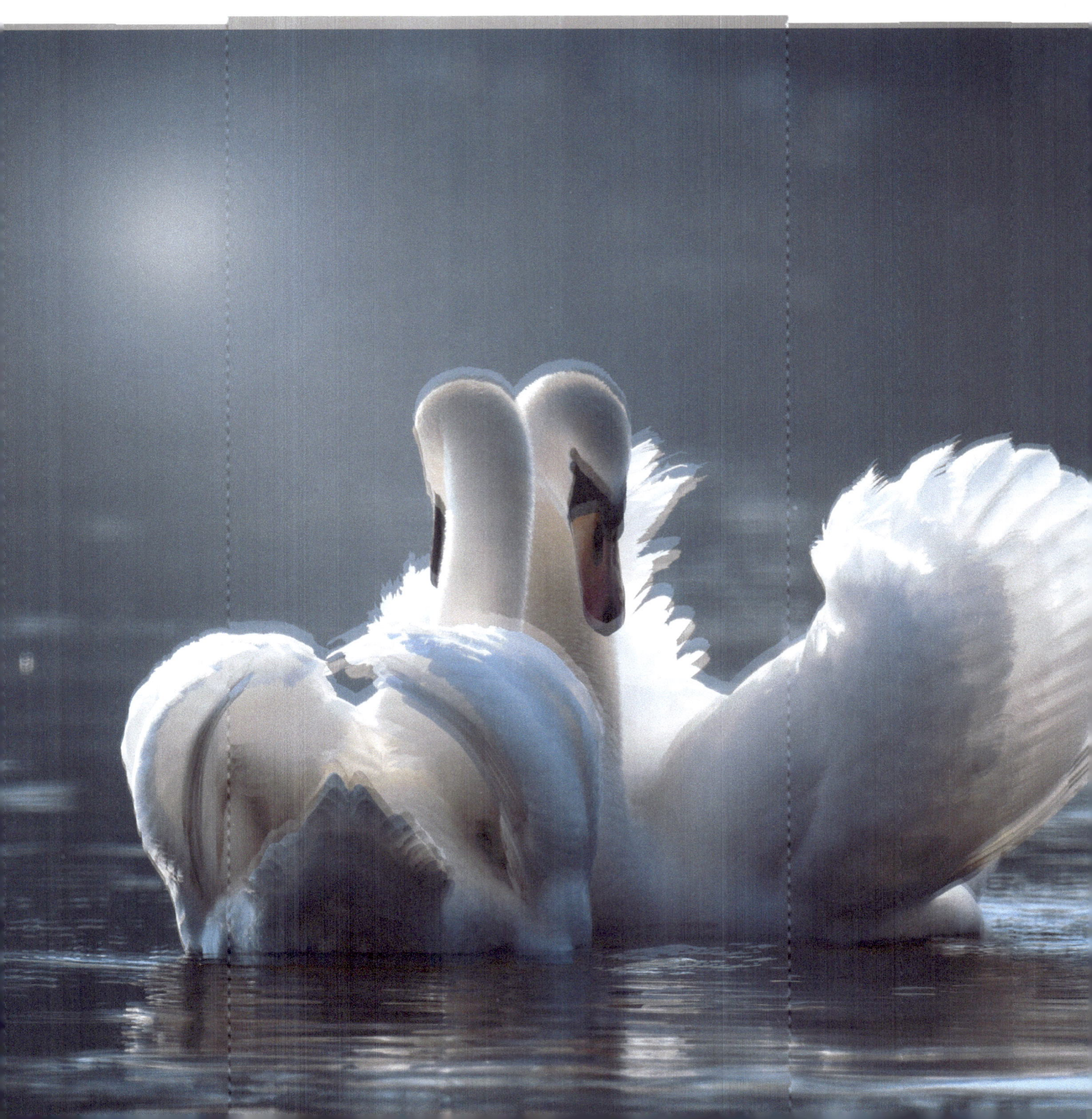

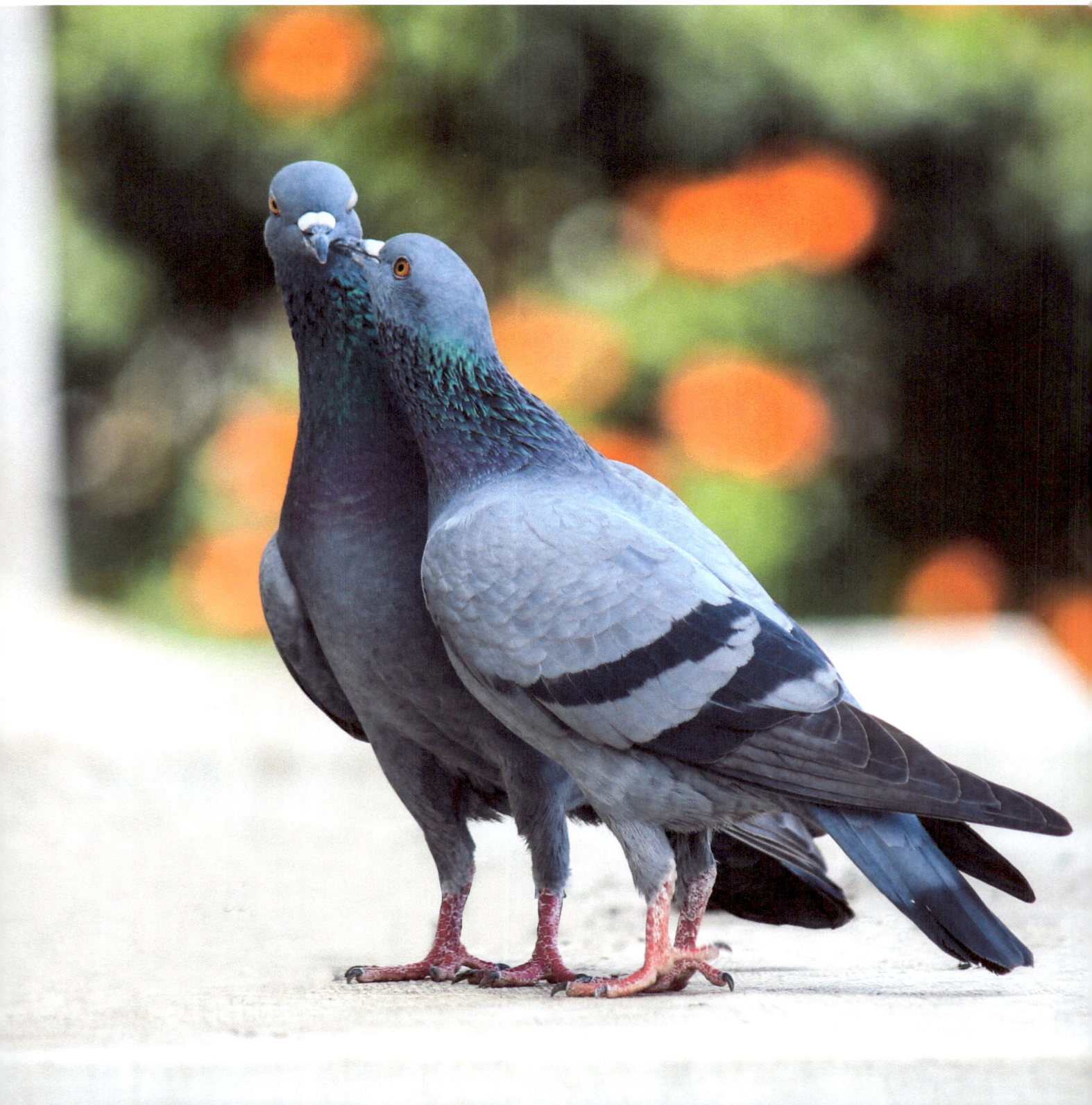

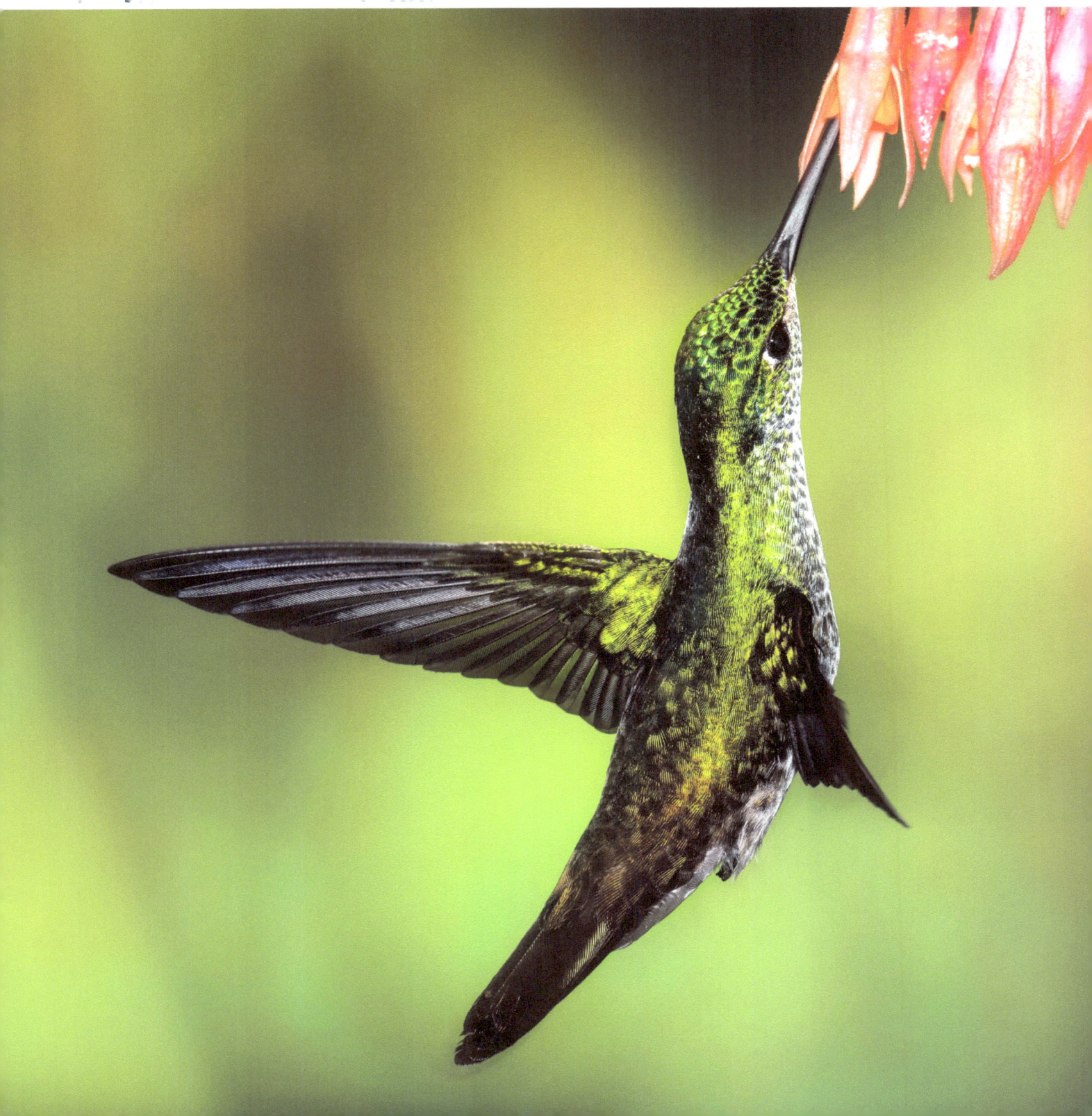

www.ingramcontent.com/pod-product-compliance
Lightning Source LLC
Chambersburg PA
CBHW051931210526
45473CB00006B/2213